Hurtling Toward
HAPPINESS

Also by Claudia Hunter Johnson

Nonfiction:

Stifled Laughter: One Woman's Story about Fighting Censorship
Crafting Short Screenplays That Connect
Script Partners: How to Succeed at Co-Writing for Film & TV
(with Matt Stevens)

Fiction:

A Christmas Belle: The Carol Continues
(with Matt Stevens)

Hurtling Toward
HAPPINESS

A MOTHER AND TEENAGE SON'S ROAD TRIP
FROM BLUES TO BONDING
IN A REALLY SMALL CAR

CLAUDIA HUNTER JOHNSON

Arcade Publishing • New York

First Edition

Arcade Publishing books may be purchased in bulk at special discounts for sales promotion, corporate gifts, fund-raising, or educational purposes. Special editions can also be created to specifications. For details, contact the Special Sales Department, Arcade Publishing, 307 West 36th Street, 11th Floor, New York, NY 10018 or arcade@skyhorsepublishing.com.

Arcade Publishing® is a registered trademark of Skyhorse Publishing, Inc.®, a Delaware corporation.

Visit our website at www.arcadepub.com.
Visit the author's website at claudiahunterjohnson.com

10 9 8 7 6 5 4 3 2 1

Library of Congress Cataloging-in-Publication Data

Names: Johnson, Claudia (Claudia Hunter), author.
Title: Hurtling toward Happiness : a mother and teenage son's road trip from blues
    to bonding in a really small car / Claudia Hunter Johnson.
Description: First edition. | New York : Arcade Publishing, 2017.
Identifiers: LCCN 2017019196| ISBN 9781628728156 (hardcover : alk. paper)
    | ISBN 9781628728170 (ebook)
Subjects: LCSH: Johnson, Claudia (Claudia Hunter)—Travel—Southern States. |
    Southern States—Description and travel. | Johnson, Claudia (Claudia
    Hunter)—Family. | Mothers and sons—United States—Biography. | Teenage
    boy—Family relationships—United States.
Classification: LCC F216.2 .J635 2017 | DDC 917.504—dc23 LC record available at
https://lccn.loc.gov/2017019196

Cover design by Erin Seaward-Hiatt
Jacket background image: iStockphoto; photograph of the author and Ross: Caroline
Pitt Loomis

Printed in the United States of America

This book is dedicated
with love and gratitude
to
my mother, Peggy Morgan Johnson, who told me our
family story;
my daughter, Anne Loomis Thompson, who told me to
record it;
and my son, Ross Johnson Loomis, who wanted to hear
it on our road trip.

Camerado, I give you my hand!

I give you my love more precious than money . . .

Will you give me yourself? Will you come travel with me?

Shall we stick by each other as long as we live?

—Walt Whitman, "Song of the Open Road"

To venture causes anxiety, but not to venture is to lose oneself.

—Søren Kierkegaard, *Sickness unto Death*

Then came spring, the great time of traveling . . .

—Jack Kerouac, *On the Road*

PART ONE

CHAPTER ONE

I-10, North Florida

April 10, 1998, Good Friday

We are hurtling west on Interstate 10, my son Ross and I, the two of us leaving our troubles behind, though the label on the side mirror cautions—OBJECTS ARE CLOSER THAN THEY APPEAR.

Ross is driving the getaway car, his slender hands on the wheel, his faux titanium Oakleys like a headband across his brown hair, but brown does not do it justice—it's brown with red highlights, a color I can't quite pin down. He's wearing his favorite T-shirt—the Death Star exploding—and green plaid seersucker shorts. Dirty socks that smell like ripe sour mash. Ratty running shoes, untied. At five eleven, he's almost too big for the gray velour seats of the small black Mystique, a compact, *el cheapo*, per our shoestring budget of $900 for the whole week (less $194.43 for this car rental). $900, or our ship is sunk.

An hour ago at Alamo Rental, Ross fell in love with their ad for an electric-blue convertible Mustang. I knew the equation—more car/less food—but, oh, I could see it, the two of us roaring down

Interstate 10 with the top down, sunburned, hair flying, and I want him to remember this trip, so I said okay. Ross did a whiplash double-take—*Mom?*—but Alamo was fresh out of Mustangs. Disappointed, we settled for this. I waxed philosophic: "The mystique of the road, and all that."

I can feel that mystique as we roll through the rolling hills of north Florida, an hour west of our home, Tallahassee. Up ahead, the road is unfolding. That's our deal—let the road trip unfold. We have no reservations, no real agenda, except to stay in New Orleans tonight with my childhood best friend, Ann Owens, now Tilton, and make it to Texas and back in a week.

Ross swerves into the left lane and passes a semi that looks like it's covered with quilted aluminum foil. I grip the gray velour armrest. He's driving too fast, but I'm trying not to say anything. He signals for the driver to honk. The driver does—two loud blasts. Ross waves and cuts back into the right lane.

My hand relaxes. "So how does it handle?"

"Like a sports car," he murmurs, and compared to the cars that he's driven, it probably does—my Mazda van and the '82 Rabbit my mother gave him when he turned sixteen. He slides his Oakleys over his eyes and shoots me a smile. Cool. The essence of cool. Tom Cruise at the beginning of *Risky Business*—*The dream is always the same.*

Ross taps cruise control.

I click my seat back a notch and settle in for the ride. It's a glorious spring afternoon—a Good Friday if ever I've seen one—a cloudless blue sky overhead, what my father, an aviator, called "the blue bowl." Pink phlox dot the Easter-green roadside. I roll down my window and breathe the cool air as we hurtle past kudzu cascading off oaks and pines that look like bears, giraffes, elephants lined up to watch us go by.

"Georgia topiary," I joke.

Ross groans. "Mom, please."

A year ago, he *liked* Georgia jokes, liked to tell them himself ("Why does the St. Johns River run north? Because Georgia *sucks!*"), but lately he's been a tough room to work, usually cutting me off before a joke's over—"*Zʒ-ʒʒt!*"—like Dr. Evil in *Austin Powers.*

"You never laugh at my jokes anymore."

"Say something funny, I will."

That hurts. I roll up the window.

We used to be close, Ross and I. Kindred spirits. The family's in-your-face comics.

"This guy calls," Ross told me last fall. "Asks for Clara. I tell him he's got the wrong number. No one named Clara lives here. And the guy *argues* with me. Like I don't know if someone named Clara lives in my house. Like I'm gonna say, 'Oh, hang on a minute, she just walked in.'"

We laughed like fools over that, but laughter has been in short supply this semester. We're both burned out, blue. Ross is burned out on school, but I suspect the burnout goes deeper. Not that he'll talk about it. We've drifted too far apart. Disconnected. I'm not even sure how it happened. Or when. There's no big blow-up to point to, no mother-son knock-down-drag-out. Our lives just slowly shifted. Continental Drift, not Big Bang. If I ask why, he clams up. I've learned not to push.

Since his sixteenth birthday last August, he's become dramatically private. His room is strictly off-limits, not that anyone in her right mind would want to walk in. The floor looks like landfill— boxer shorts, books, crumpled homework, an impressive assortment of Frisbees, a guitar, and a wrench. I've cracked CDs and snapped off his boom-box antenna trying to cross the floor to kiss him goodnight, but that's how he seems to want it—minimal physical contact—except when he ambushes me in the hall and throws me over his shoulder and shouts, "Torture Rack!"—his favorite World Wide Wrestling hold. But heaven forbid I should give him a kiss or squeeze his upper arm and admire the muscles he's developed since he started pole-vaulting and playing Ultimate Frisbee.

The last time I squeezed his arm we were in Walmart, standing in line. A Saturday. Crowded. Without thinking, I squeezed his arm, and he said, nice and loud, "*Mom!* I don't want to be touched in that way." People stared. Someone hissed, "Sicko!"

So I don't press him for answers, but I hate the way we've drifted apart. Now, for instance, in this cramped compact car, our shoulders are an inch apart, max, almost touching (though I don't plan on pointing that out), yet the distance between us has never felt greater. I hardly know who he *is* anymore.

I look over at him, squinting into the afternoon sun—my own son but a mystery to me—and I'm overwhelmed with a yearning to be close again. That's why I've come on this trip—to be closer, connect—but I also know that it could backfire. This cooped-up closeness could drive us further apart.

We've had our worst fights in cars. Ross speeds, takes curves too fast, tailgates. If I say anything, he freaks out, drives faster. And God help me if I try to play music. He *hates* the music I like. Oldies are bad enough—*moldy oldies*, he calls them—but if I put on classical music or Emmylou Harris, he shrieks and covers his ears. I feel the same way when I hear his music—rap, heavy metal. I've been known to shout, "Am I in *hell?*"

Not to mention we'll be sharing motel rooms. He's a night crawler. I'm a drooling zombie by ten.

Ross speeds up again. I glance at the speedometer—eighty. He's bearing down on a baby-blue semi with WERNER written across it in foot-high gold letters. A small sign on the back—HOW'S MY DRIVING?—is getting bigger and bigger.

"Don't tailgate!" I snap. It slips out before I can stop it.

"*Mom!*" he barks back. Like every other male on the planet, he hates backseat driving. If I say "Don't tailgate," he hears "You suck." He speeds up. "This is *nothing*. You should see how Mouth drives."

Mouth is Ross's mentor on Florida State University's Ultimate team—Demented Ultimate Freaks—a name I'm beginning to think they deserve.

"When we drive to tournaments, Mouth gets right *behind* semis. I mean, *inches* away."

"With you in the car?"

"It's called drafting," Ross says, as if that makes it okay. "Cuts down wind resistance. Saves on gas mileage."

I cover my face. You send your kid out in the world, let him play on FSU's Ultimate team even though he's sixteen because he's that gifted a player and the sport seems to be the only thing that he loves. You entrust him to others who assure you there won't be any drinking or drugs, then you find out the question you should have been asking is HOW'S YOUR DRIVING?

"Here, I'll show you," Ross says.

"Please don't!" I take me hands off my face.

He speeds up. Eighty-one, eighty-two . . .

"Slow down!"

"I know what I'm doing!"

"You've had your license six months!"

"Eight!" He moves into the shadow cast behind the truck

heading into the afternoon sun. We're little more than a car length away. The Mystique sits so low we're eye level with the semi's red-and-white bumper. If the truck slows down or brakes, we're decapitated.

"Ross, stop it. You're going to kill us!"

"I'm not gonna kill us!"

I close my eyes and try to stay calm. Last year, at Busch Gardens, I agreed to ride the big roller coasters (I *hate* roller coasters), Kumba and Montu—the *front row* of Montu—to show Ross I wasn't a wimp. I survived the sickening *click click click click* as we slowly climbed to the top before plunging so fast it felt like being slam-dunked by God, but that didn't prepare me for this—flying down an Interstate highway in a tin can of a car that's kissing a semi's back bumper.

I open my eyes, see the small sign on the back of the truck—IF YOU CAN'T SEE MY MIRRORS, I CAN'T SEE YOU. I can see mud flaps flapping. I see bits of dried mud hitting our windshield—*thwack thwack!* I see where the tread's worn away on the semi's back tires. But I can't see his mirrors. My heart goes *squish squish.*

Ross takes his foot off the gas, but our speed doesn't change. "See, Mom, we're drafting."

I lose it. "*You're scaring the shit out of me!*"

Now he laughs. Shoots me a look—*gotcha!* And I realize I've just lost a round of mother-son chicken.

He slows down, dropping back. "Okay, no more drafting." But he still has that wicked look on his face—*Ya big wimp. Weenie. Wuss.*

I watch the Werner truck barrel into the distance. I think, *I won't survive this. Was I out of my mind? A week on the road with a teen? What the hell was I thinking?*

I want to say, "Turn around, turn over the keys," but I don't. I take a deep breath and let it out slowly. I'm not giving up on this road trip—our first and maybe our last. I'm going the distance if it kills us both.

Ross resumes a comfortable speed and taps cruise control. Cool. The essence of cool.

I feel the color return to my face.

He shoots me a smile. "You've got to lighten up, Mom. It's spring break."

Then he whoops, grabs my hand, and holds it up high, like Thelma and Louise just before they fly over the cliff.

"We're doing it, Mom! We're going to Texas!"

CHAPTER TWO

Tallahassee

The idea for the road trip came out of the blue. Or the blues, I should say.

Ten days ago, having dinner, Ross announced he was leaving. Only a sophomore, he said he wanted to graduate early from his high school—Maclay—and go to college at the end of his junior year.

Other parents might rejoice at the news—*one less year with a teen!*—but to me it sounded like an alarm. I felt like I was waking up, struggling through layers of sleep, life, preoccupation, until the moment came into focus—Ross telling me he'd be gone in a year.

I set down my fork, carefully lining it up with the edge of my placemat. "Why?" I asked, feigning calm.

Ross shrugged and looked down at his plate, his face hidden behind a brown curtain of hair.

"Will you have enough credits?"

"Yeah," he answered, monosyllabic. "I think so," he added, expansive.

"I want you to make this decision with full information," I said, sounding like some prim asshole when I wanted to shout, *You can't go! I've hardly seen you this year!*

Here's what I know—you can love a child fiercely and not even see him. *Really* see him. Our lives get too hectic. We put our children on hold—*Your life is important to me, so if you'll leave your name and number, I'll get back to you as soon as I can.* And we assume they'll still be here when we do.

I looked at Ross across my plate of Szechuan stir-fry. It was the last day of March and it felt like the first time I'd seen him all year.

He met my gaze, his eyes green, cool, decided.

The passage was coming, and I wasn't ready. Oh, I knew leaving home was the natural order of things—my daughter, Anne, was a junior at Dartmouth—but not a year *early*. Not when we'd drifted so far apart. *If he leaves while we're disconnected, I'll lose him for good.* The thought made me want to howl at the half-moon I saw out the window—*I need a lost-and-found for the people I love!*

Three years ago—the year Anne left for Dartmouth—my father died. Colon cancer. Three hundred sixty-five days after his diagnosis—a long, sad, bittersweet year.

Two years ago, my mother had a small stroke, manifested by double vision. Last summer, she had a second. I'd just returned from a trip to Atlanta and called to tell her I was home safely. Stop the meter on her worrying. She's a world-class worrier, my mother, and she was relieved that I'd called. She was talking a blue streak when, mid-sentence, her words turned to gobbledygook. Strange syllables in a familiar sentence-like structure. *Dear God*, I thought, *my mother is dying*. I finally managed to say, "Mom, I think you're having a stroke."

"Ga ba da ba ga?" she said.

An MRI revealed a 50 to 70 percent blockage in her left carotid artery. Her vascular surgeon, Dr. Lawhorn—a gentle, soft-spoken Southerner—explained that it was cause for concern but not surgery. He'd scan her again in six months.

Miraculously, she recovered her speech in a month, but last fall she began to have memory lapses. She's always been the Queen of Can-Do—*The hell it won't fit! Give me a bigger hammer!*—but the smallest things started to overwhelm her. Working her TV remote. Keeping her prescriptions straight. Grocery shopping. Or she'd call to ask me what day it was. Then, toward the end of last year, her behavior became, well, a little bizarre. One evening, when her neighbors across her back privacy fence threw a garden party and played music too loud, in my mother's opinion, she turned on the faucet and hosed down the guests until they turned down the music.

"How late was it?" I asked when she told me.

"Late!" she said. "Ten o'clock!"

"She's slipping," I told Ross, who didn't believe me until late December when she called him four times in a row to thank him for the same Christmas present.

In January, I took a sabbatical from teaching screenwriting at the Florida State Film School so I could jump-start my stalled-out writing career. My best-laid plan was to write a book about Ruby McCollum, the wealthiest African-American woman in Live Oak, Florida, wife of Bolita Sam, who ran the illegal lottery-style gambling racket known as bolita (Spanish for "little ball") in town. A well-educated mother of four with a fifth on the way, Ruby was convicted of first-degree murder and sentenced to the electric chair for the 1952 murder of her white doctor and alleged lover, State Senator-elect Dr. Clifford LeRoy Adams, Jr.

News of the interracial murder rocked the nation, the state, and the region, escalating racial tension in Live Oak that remains to this day, where it's still an unbelievably controversial hot topic in town. This story they do not want told.

But I'm an ardent advocate for free speech, the First Amendment, and I connected deeply to Ruby's story in 1991 when I discovered that the white power structure had silenced her on the stand and to the press. Zora Neale Hurston, who covered the trial for the *Pittsburgh Courier*, concluded that "the truth lay on the other side of silence." For seven years I've been doing research, trying to penetrate the hostile and mysterious silence surrounding Ruby's story and find out why she was silenced and why she killed LeRoy Adams.

She didn't, I discovered last fall when two courageous African-Americans—Doug Udell and Corinne Morris—risked everything and broke their long silence. Ruby was framed by Live Oak's white power structure to protect one of their own and cover up their corruption. Corruption confirmed by my key white informant, Julian Roberts, son of state representative Houston Roberts, who, like other politicos—and law enforcement—had taken bolita payoffs for years.

Uncovering this startling new information—buried by Live Oak's corrupt white power structure for forty-six years—was a breathtaking breakthrough that might rewrite history and right a terrible wrong. So my sabbatical could not have come at a more perfect time.

"Oh, really?" the Cosmic Ironist said.

Or, as Virgil says in Ross's Latin textbook, "It seemed otherwise to the gods."

When I took my mother in for her second carotid artery scan,

Dr. Lawhorn placed his stethoscope on the left side of her neck, listened, frowned, and listened again. He heard no *whoosh-whoosh*, no blood rushing up to her brain. The artery was 99 percent blocked.

"Well, Peggy, he said kindly, "your brain's getting half the blood that it needs. It's like a muffler pipe stuffed with a potato."

My mother sat there, more serene than I'd seen her in years. Numbed by the news, I asked why the left carotid was blocked but the right artery wasn't.

Dr. Lawhorn shook his gray head. "If I knew the answer to that, I'd win the Nobel Prize." He scheduled surgery for the following Monday, a risky procedure—he would open her neck, clamp the artery above and below the clogged section, then he had four minutes—*four minutes!*—someone stood by with a stopwatch—to clean it out, sew it up, and take the clamps off. Four minutes, or that's all she wrote.

That was all I wrote, too, for a while, except in my journal: *Most important, most on my mind—Mom's surgery. I haven't head-on acknowledged my fears, but, oh they are there—a great anxiety field that she might not come through it.*

This pushed a whole panel of buttons for me. I'd been getting over my father's death slowly, if you ever get over the loss of a parent. I would still be broadsided by grief when I saw someone with a distinguished white beard or heard music my father loved— *The Mikado, HMS Pinafore,* Sousa marches—but the waves of grief were hitting less often. Then Dr. Lawhorn heard no *whoosh-whoosh*, and oh, the waves started rolling again.

That night I dreamed that I needed something done to my brain. The doctor wasn't sure what it was, so I got a second opinion. The second doctor didn't know either; he just candidly told me he needed the money. I was scared and confused until Ross appeared in my dream and informed me that a third surgeon would carve my name in my shaved scalp for identification, and—ah, dreams!—this was a *plus*.

I told Ross about the dream over breakfast, and he pointed out that it was a perfect combo of Mimaw's surgery, brain, and my own midlife desperation to have my name carved into *something*.

I cocked a half smile, impressed, though a little unnerved that he read me so loud and clear. "When did you get so smart?"

"It's so obvious, Mom," he said, as if I were the dumbest broad on the planet.

At least we were talking. Most of the time we'd pass in the hall, toss off a "How are you?" But I seldom stuck around for the answer. I was so caught up in my mother's condition I hardly saw Ross, except the night before Mom's surgery, at Maclay's production of *Cinderella*. Ross played the Prince. I leaned forward in my folding chair, dumbstruck by how handsome he was, so lanky and tall, almost six feet in the black rubber boots he was wearing. I thought, *He's my child?* He seemed so grown up, so distant from me, and I realized as he danced center stage—a touch gawky but, yes, charming—that we were going through the same thing. Separating. Saying goodbye to our mothers.

My mother and I have always been close. Two tomboys from Texas. On Monday morning, before dawn, before Tallahassee's abundance of birds began to wake up, I sat in her hospital room, the two of us laughing about the rascals we'd been. When she was six, in San Antonio, she climbed a pecan tree and shouted, "Chicken shit!" at the kids in her neighborhood. When I was seven, in Corpus Christi, I set up a penny-toss casino board and fleeced all the kids in mine, though she made me return all their money.

A cheerful nurse appeared and said it was time for surgical prep. I kissed my mother's lined cheek, soft as powder.

She smiled, far less upset about this procedure than I was. "I've had a good life," she said, trying to stop the meter on my worrying. "Sixty-nine years."

I nodded.

The nurse administered drugs—coffee for me and morphine for Mom—and I watched my mother depart "on Fellini Airlines," as Ross likes to say.

"It scares me that you know that," I told him the first time he said it.

"We live in a drug culture, Mom."

My mother has the bluest eyes, the color of pale stonewashed denim. Perfectly round. Big as nickels. As a black orderly pushed her gurney down the long fluorescent-lit hallway, she gazed up at his face and said dreamily, "Black people have the prettiest skin. I used to love to paint blacks for that reason." It was true—her painting of a black gambler rolling dice ("Luck, Be a Lady Tonight") hangs in her living room, but I fell a few steps behind, pretending I didn't hear her.

The orderly stopped. "This is surgical prep."

It took me a moment to grasp what he meant: *This is as far as you go, the end of the line.*

For me, not for her, please, please not for her, I thought as I kissed her cool forehead. *Luck, be a lady today.*

Mom patted my cheek. And disappeared through the door.

Like a soul in Limbo, I drifted through the halls, sighing, until Dr. Lawhorn appeared in his pistachio-green surgical scrubs.

I snapped at him, "Yes?" I'm pretty sure that I snapped at the man.

He smiled. "Everything's fine."

Mom went home the next morning—modern medicine's miracle woman. The color returned to her cheeks, but she still had memory lapses. Her memory—and the shared past between us—seemed to be fading.

At her two-week checkup, I took Dr. Lawhorn aside and asked the dread question, "Is it Alzheimer's disease?"

"I don't think so," he said. "But there's dementia."

When I got home, I looked up the definition: *Irreversible deterioration of intellectual faculties resulting from organic brain disorder.*

Irreversible.

It probably isn't Alzheimer's, I wrote in my journal, *and there's some comfort in that, but this is—next to Dad dying of cancer—the most painful process I've had to watch—such a brilliant woman, a historian no less, forgetting, forgetting.*

By the end of January, I'd barely unpacked my Ruby research, much less started writing the book. Then, on the morning of January 26, I got a call from Julian Roberts, who asked if I'd meet him that night at the Brown Lantern restaurant in Live Oak. He had something to tell me that he couldn't tell me over the phone.

I left a note for Ross and a plate of food in the fridge and drove east on I-10 to Live Oak, still a deceptively sleepy town on the Suwannee River, and joined Julian in the corner booth at the Brown Lantern beneath the skin of a six-foot timber rattler nailed vertically up the wall—the perfect place for what he was about to tell me.

A waitress brought us two Coronas with wedges of lime tucked in the top. The place was crowded and noisy with conversation and the *ding-ding-ding* of pinball machines.

Even so, Julian lowered his voice. "A friend of mine who's high up in law enforcement—I won't tell you his name because we go way back—asked me to let you know that there's been 'a gathering.'"

I jammed the wedge of lime into the neck of my beer. "A *gathering?*"

"Your name came up and the fact that you're making a film and writing a book about Ruby McCollum, and, basically, they'll stop at nothing to silence you."

"Oh, I love it," I laughed, a tense little outburst. "A death threat from the people paid to protect you!"

Julian smiled with a knowing sadness.

I picked up my beer. Took a sip. Tasted lime. "Do you think I should be worried about this?"

He nodded. "There's a criminal element in town who could get it done."

Get it done. The words hung in the brief silence between us.

"When my best friend turned State's witness in a drug trial here a few years ago, he was murdered."

"God, Julian, I'm so sorry."

"I mailed myself a letter before I came here tonight, in case anything happened."

I studied his pale poet's face. "So what should I do?"

"Lie low," he said gently. "The interviews are done. Just put it away for a while."

Driving home on I-10, I felt everything I cared about slipping away. My family. My work. *Seven years of research up in smoke!* But

I would not—would *not*—write the book while Ross was at home. I could risk my life, but not his. Never his.

No, I was done. And not just with Ruby. With writing.

Talk about *vertigo*. I'd lost my bearings, my sense of balance. I felt like Dante who woke up "in a dark wood where the right road was wholly lost and gone." The right road for me had always been writing. I'd wanted to write since I was ten. I'd built my whole life around this desire, but now it was gone. For the life of me I couldn't remember why I'd wanted to write or why I would ever want to do it again.

What I *wanted* to do was keep driving west on Interstate 10, or better yet, take a bus, let someone else do the driving, but just keep going, past Tallahassee, get away from it all—death threats, dementia, disconnection. I played the scenario over and over as I hurtled west under the star-resplendent night sky, and by the time I pulled into our driveway, I was in the middle of a full-blown escape fantasy.

Ross was already asleep, fully clothed, on his bed, surrounded by homework. I carefully crossed his bedroom-floor landfill, set his homework aside, and covered him with his blue Maclay blanket. I kissed the tips of my fingers and touched his troubled forehead. I turned off the light and went to my study.

I sat at my desk in the moonlight, surrounded by piles of Ruby research. I wondered what others did when their dreams ran out of gas. My mother dreamed of a long, happy marriage. My father dreamed of a long, happy *life*.

"Sometimes you have to pack up your dreams and put them up on a shelf," my mother has said many times since I was a girl, and I've always disagreed passionately with her. Now it made sense.

I picked up the phone and called Julian. "Tell your friend that I got the message. I'm bagging the film and the book."

I found three empty boxes in the garage and threw in all my research for the book—audio and video interview tapes, transcriptions, court transcripts, books, articles, newspaper clippings, microfilm, manuscript pages—and I sealed the boxes with clear packing tape, sealed them with a vengeance, like a murderer sealing the mouths of her victims. And staggering slightly under the weight, I carried the boxes back to the garage and shoved them in an open space on a shelf.

They fit just right.

Over breakfast the next morning, I told Ross I'd quit.

"I'm glad," he said. "That project sucked."

"No, I've quit writing."

He swiped his orange juice off the table, took a swig, slammed it down. "Mom," he said, "it's your *bliss*." A word he doesn't take lightly.

Last year I gave the commencement address at Maclay. I told the students to follow their bliss. "Be who thou art," I said, quoting Nietzsche. Ross heard those words and believed them. He believed I believed them, and I did when I said them. But now it was clear from the look on his face that he thought I was a big fat hypocrite and this was a rotten decision that would only increase the distance between us—but what could I say?

"No, it's not my bliss anymore."

He fake-sneezed *loser* and sat there glaring at me, a string of snot hanging out of his nose.

Anne was a bit more supportive. When I emailed her at Dartmouth and told her I'd quit, she shot back a wry answer:

I think you need and deserve a break. How long have you been doing this? Like 20 years? Remember that breaks are important. I think it was Copernicus (but maybe it was Galileo) who couldn't figure out some problem about the orbit of Mars and set it aside for 7 or 15 years and came back and solved it right away. A good lesson, eh?

She urged me to spend some of my sabbatical collecting *our* family story instead of Ruby McCollum's. Before Mimaw's memory was gone for good.

I took her advice. I went to Mom's house and told her I wanted to talk, really talk, about our time in Texas—good, bad, and ugly. She was surprised and delighted—I usually changed the subject when she talked about the darker side of the story. But this time I listened—and tape-recorded—as she told me about the sins of her father, Alden Webb Morgan—Granddaddy, I called him—a brilliant but tormented man, a self-taught engineer with auburn hair and gray-blue eyes that changed when he drank.

"A line would appear in his jaw, then his eyes would turn a steely cold blue," she told me. "His eyes would have a murderous gaze. Daddy had vicious guilt when he drank, so he had to blame someone and it was usually Mother. He would fly into a rage, hit her over and over, smashing her face beyond recognition until there was blood on his hands. Then he'd go on long crying jags, apologize, and the cycle would start all over again."

She told me about his childhood in Texas as well as her mother's—Mamaw, I called her. She told me about their courtship and marriage, how Mamaw divorced him twice in the forties but always went back. I asked why.

"She was in her early forties, a beautiful woman with so much potential, but he said, 'I'll come after you and kill you wherever you are. No matter where you go, I'll track you down and kill you.'

Well, what do you do with a man like that? There ought to be a law that you can kill him, because she couldn't win. But on the other hand, why did she marry him? She knew he was a horrible bully."

Mom told me about her Texas childhood. She told me about marrying my naval aviator father when she was seventeen, in part to get away from her father. She said she didn't fall in love with my father until the day I was born, but the marriage fell apart anyway, and she and my sister and I moved back to Texas so she could be close to her sister—my Aunt Patty—and her two sons—my first cousins, Jeff and Jon—and Mamaw and Granddaddy. I was six.

Through February and March I went to her house every day, tape recorder in tow, and documented the dramatic sweep of our family story, my mother stopping sometimes, overcome with emotion, with tears in her eyes. "There are so many stories that weave together."

It was a balmy spring morning, March 3rd, when she finished, recounting a part I knew well and loved hearing again—how she and my big sister, Patty, and I drove north out of Kingsville, leaving Texas for good. I was about to be a sophomore in high school.

Like Ross.

While I listened, I sat on the grass in her backyard and cut back the brittle brown growth of her old Boston fern. Underneath, tiny ferns were curled up, tender green commas, quotation marks. Trimming the plant I felt the oddest sensation—bliss—and I thought of Jung's midlife realization that his career had made him one-sided, cerebral—"with much Self-potential falling into the unconscious," as he put it.

Psychic road kill, I thought, tossing the brown growth aside. I wondered what Self-potential I'd lost in my twenty-plus years of being a writer. But I was far more concerned about what

Self-potential Ross might be losing. The latest research I'd been reading about mothers and sons said a close, warm relationship between them predicts, as nothing else can, the son's self-confidence, independence, and success forming loving relationships in later life. But when mothers and sons drift apart, the son loses touch not just with his mother—he loses touch with important parts of himself.

That evening, Ross announced he'd be leaving Maclay a year early. We left the table in silence and sat in the living room, reading.

It was late evening—"the blue hour," as my mother used to call it in Texas. Ross sprawled across the love seat, his long skinny feet sticking off of the armrest. I leaned back in the beige recliner I'd inherited from my father, reading another book about mothers and sons. This one said that the sadness of those who drift apart is deep, universal, and lasts their whole lifetime.

I looked at Ross, listlessly turning the pages of his Latin textbook. When he was in middle school, my friend Bonnie asked him, "If you could only do one thing to achieve world peace, what would it be?

"Get to the parents," Ross answered. "Teach them how to be good parents."

Since I was a ten-year-old tomboy in Texas, I've only wanted two things—to be a mother and a writer—and I felt like a total failure at both. My life felt like a low-down dirty trick. I felt an overwhelming desire to be close to Ross, but I didn't know where to begin, so I fantasized about boarding that bus and heading west on Interstate 10. The evening showing of my escape fantasy.

Ross sighed and shifted position. "You know what I'd like to do?"

My fantasy stopped. "What?" I said.

"I'd like to get on I-10 and drive west."

I gaped—*We have the same escape fantasy? What was this, genetic?* "You have that fantasy, too?"

He sat up. "All the time."

"Me, too," I said, sympathetic.

He snorted. "No way."

"Way," I assured him, closing my book.

We compared notes. In my fantasy, I rode a bus. In his, he drove.

"So," he said, "can I do it?"

"Do what?"

"Drive west on Interstate 10."

"Whoa now, just a minute. I thought we were talking fantasy here."

"I want to go, Mom. For spring break."

My maternal instincts kicked in. "Well, you can't. You're too young."

"I'm sixteen!"

"Exactly!"

"God, Mom!" He was standing now, all five feet eleven.

"You've only been driving six months."

"Eight!"

"Anne drove before she was ready and totaled a car."

"I'm not Anne!" He raked his brown hair.

"No, forget it," I said, feeling steamrolled.

"Mom, I'll be fine!"

"You're not taking off by yourself."

"Then come with me."

"Oh, right." Then I saw the fierce look on his face and realized that he wasn't kidding. "You want to spend spring break with your *mother?*"

"It'd be awesome, Mom. We could drive to LA."

"That's five days each direction. You only have seven." As if I were even considering going.

"Then we'll find someplace in between!" He wheeled around to the bookcase and opened our atlas, stabbing the USA map with his index finger. "We could go to Texas!"

I laughed. "Texas?"

"We could see the Alamo, then we could hit Kingsville." He showed me the map, the red east-west line for Interstate 10. Sure enough, San Antonio was smack in the middle. "How long has it been since you've been to Kingsville?"

"A long time," I said, doing a quick calculation. "Thirty-two years."

"Let's do it, Mom," he said, looking at me. "Let's go see your old trotting ground."

"Ross, no, this is nuts." What if we ended up hating each other? My worst fear would come true—he'd leave home and *never* come back. But we did have the same escape fantasy. Maybe this trip was meant to be. And I knew it would be the last time he'd ask. A last chance. If I didn't take it, I'd probably lose the boy anyway. "Okay," I told him.

He hooted. "You mean it?"

"I do."

He flopped on the love seat and studied the map, marveling at the miles that we'd travel. "Two thousand miles in one week!"

But the only distance I cared about was the distance between us.

April 10, 1998, Good Friday

Total trip budget: **$900.00**

Alamo Rental: −$194.43

Balance remaining: **$705.57**

CHAPTER THREE

I-10, Florida Panhandle

Across the armpit of Florida we go, into the Marianna Lowlands that extend sixty miles to the Choctawhatchee River.

Still driving, Ross is grousing about our meeting last Wednesday with Maclay's academic adviser, Mr. Webster. We sat in chairs in front of his paper-strewn desk while Ross explained that he wanted to graduate a year early.

A curmudgeon with blue eyes and a basso profundo, Mr. Webster scowled. "I don't want to discourage you, Ross, but I have to be honest—we don't recommend it. Where are you thinking of going to college?"

"Brown or Stanford," Ross said.

"You'll never get in as a junior," Mr. Webster said bluntly. He softened a little. "Well, *you* might but you won't be mature enough to get through. We've sent five students early to college and all five failed."

Ross shrugged, unfazed. "Then I'll graduate early and take a year off."

"And do what?" asked Mr. Webster.

"Travel. Kick around Europe."

I gazed at Ross. "And who's paying for this?"

A long silence.

"So," Ross said, "do I have enough credits?"

Mr. Webster studied the transcripts, frowning. "Yes," he said, "you do."

Now, heading west on I-10, Ross channels Mr. Webster's deep voice. "I don't want to discourage you, Ross." A perfect mimic, then he drops it. "And he spent the next hour discouraging me!"

I brighten. "Are you discouraged?"

"*Puh!*" he says, an exclamation I can only approximate here. A small explosion of irritation, contempt. A *p-pop*. A bilabial fricative, as linguists would say. "It just makes me want to graduate sooner. I wish I could leave at the end of *this* year."

"You can't just throw in the towel."

Ross looks at me. "You did."

We drive on in silence that isn't really silence at all. The tires *flap flap flap* on this patchwork section of Interstate 10.

I can tell by the set of his jaw he's still angry at me for abandoning what once was my bliss, but I've tried to explain that it's working out for the best. The day after I boxed up my Ruby research, I got an email from a former student, Kelly Rouse, in LA:

The production company I work for, Echo Lake, wants to hire a consultant to find public domain books and plays to develop for film. Do you know anyone?

I shot back, *Yes! Hire me!* I reminded her that I had a PhD in English with a major in drama and a minor in film. She was blown away I'd consider the job.

Her boss, Doug Mankoff, liked the idea. He liked my credentials. I liked Echo Lake's mission statement: "Telling compelling, relevant, timeless stories and helping independent filmmakers make films that matter." He and I had our first telephone interview yesterday, and we clicked right away. We discovered we're both from Texas.

"The only two liberals from Texas," he laughed. He said he'd need a few days to figure out how long he'd need me and how much he could pay. We scheduled a second phone interview for this coming Tuesday, April 14, at one o'clock sharp, LA time.

"Terrific," I said. "I'll call you from somewhere in Texas."

Texas. This rented Mystique may feel like a sports car to Ross, but to me it feels like a shiny black time machine heading simultaneously for my past and my future, a peculiar sensation, like walking up a down escalator. Santa Monica lies at the opposite end of Interstate 10. If things work out, I'll fly to LA and be a consultant for Echo Lake for a few weeks in May. If we click, I might join them full time. In a year. After Ross leaves for college. I would never uproot him, make him reinvent himself his last year in high school, while I'm busy reinventing myself.

Once, a few years ago in LA, I had lunch with a successful TV writer/producer, a friend of a friend. As we were leaving the Delmonico Grill, we talked about family. He had a daughter, but when she was a girl he and his wife were so busy building careers they hardly saw her. She ran away when she was a teen—drugs, prostitution, the whole horror story. He stood there gazing down La Cienega Boulevard. "We lost her," he said.

The *flap flap flap* stops as the road's surface smooths out again.

"Ross," I say, "sometimes people quit." *Like you*, I'd like to say, but I don't.

"Yeah, well, people are *stupid*."

"And I'm not quitting writing completely."

He shoots me a skeptical look—*oh, yeah, right.*

"I'll still be working with writing at Echo Lake."

"But it won't be your own."

My jaw feels tight as frustration rises—*why won't he let me off the hook?* I consider telling him about the death threat, but I don't because he won't understand, not until he's a parent. He'll think I'm a coward. "I'm just changing directions."

"Me, too. I'm not quitting school, I'm just moving on."

A year early, I think but don't say. Since he announced he was leaving, some inner wisdom has warned me to stay out. *If you make him stay for his senior year and he hates it, he'll hate you, too.* "It's your decision."

"Good," he says, "because I've decided."

"I just wish I could understand why."

He looks at me warily, weighing the risks of opening up. "School sucks. My classes are boring as *piss*."

There's a blink in the sunlight as we shoot under an overpass.

"You like biology, right?"

"I *love* biology."

"You're going to win the biology medal."

"Jesus, Mom, I don't care about medals! I care about *science*, but after physics next year, there's nothing to take."

"The curriculum runs out?"

"Yes. At Maclay."

"Surely one of your teachers will do an independent study with you."

"Surely they won't," he assures me.

"And stop calling me Shirley." Ba *dum*. Another joke bites the dust. "What about Florida State? Dual enrollment?"

"Mom!" he snaps, as if I'm deliberately missing the point. "I want to hang with people my *age*."

"You like the Demented Ultimate Freaks."

"They're great guys, but I can't drink with them, can I?"

"Well, no, that's our deal," I say, thrown by this curve ball. Is this conversation about alcohol? Does he want permission to drink? At sixteen?

"And I've kept my promise," Ross says, "but it means I can't party with them."

"No, it means you can't drink."

"*Mom*." His eyes say *how dumb can you get?* "It's great the guys let me play, it's a real honor, but they're not my peer group. Kids need a peer group. You've heard of that, right?"

"Hey," I say, stung, "you're the one who wanted to play with the FSU men's club."

"I *do* want to play," he says, almost shouting. "I *love* Ultimate. More than anything else in the world." *Including you*, says the short pause that follows. "But I want to play it with *friends*. I can do that at Stanford or Brown."

If you get in, I think but don't say. "What about your friends at Maclay?"

His face clouds. "What friends?" He swings into the left lane and passes a slow U-Haul truck. Best Move for the Money it says on the side. "I feel trapped," he says. "I'm loved everywhere but my school."

"Ross—" I start to protest because I know it's not true. He's been loved at Maclay since he arrived in sixth grade. And he's had a great group of good friends, twelve guys, including Ross. The Dirty Dozen, I call them. But I also know not to argue with what someone's feeling. "Do you want to talk about it?"

He snorts. "*No.*"

"Anne says we talk about everything over dinner *except* our feelings."

Ross screws up his face and lets loose a mock sob. "Oh, I'm feeling so *baaaad,*" then he drops it and says, "Pass the salt."

A perfect portrait of our family dynamic—mask emotion with comedy—and I'd laugh if I didn't feel so weary, wrung out.

He slows down for construction, the Mystique tilting on uneven pavement. "Okay, chick flick's over. Time for Clive Cussler."

"Oh, let's not," I say.

Yesterday, Ross said I had to bring a Cussler novel on tape. "Techno-thriller shit?" I asked him. Tales of male prowess just aren't my bag. Granddaddy used to keep stacks of *Argosy* magazines in his bathroom in Corpus Christi when I was a girl. I'd flip through them, a little disturbed by the illustrations of cowering big-breasted women caught in the cross-hairs of some hunter's rifle. "Just do it, Mom," Ross insisted. So I went to the public library and checked out Clive Cussler's *Shock Wave* and some guidebooks for Louisiana and Texas.

He cuts me a look. "Mom, you promised."

I produce on my face an innocent look. "Did I?"

"Before we left Tallahassee. You promised you'd listen."

He's got me there, and I've learned never to break a promise with Ross. I've never seen anyone feel so let down, betrayed. I make a mental note to be more careful about what I promise. "Yeah, right, okay."

I reach behind his seat and rummage in the canvas book bag

on the back seat while Ross fills me in about Cussler's hero, Dirk Pitt—a former Navy Seal with savoir-faire and technical savvy. "Just think of him as an underwater James Bond."

"Terrific," I say. *Tits and ass*. I pull *Shock Wave* out of the bag and think wistfully of all those years I spent reading to Ross—the nights by the wood-burning stove at our farm in Live Oak reading *To Kill a Mockingbird*. The hot afternoons in our two-person hammock taking turns reading aloud from Roahl Dahl's *The Witches* or Dahl's luminous stories, "The Pickpocket" and "The Swan." The years it took to read him all seven Narnia books. And it's all come to this—*Shock Wave*. "Jesus, when did you get to be such a guy?"

Ross lifts his foot off the gas—the car lurches slightly—then he speeds up again.

Uh-oh, I think. *I've done it again.*

"You know, Mom," he says. "I like being a guy. I *like* it. Sitting around with other guys watching a game and scratching myself. Just hanging out. Peeing standing up. Not have to worry about my appearance and similar *shiʒnit*." The fierce look has returned to his face, as if he's declaring his independence.

I realize he is. He's drawing a line in the sand. Demanding respect. And I feel mine rising for him, for this stand he's just taken. We tend to dump on men in this family, my mother and I, even Anne at times, but especially Mom, and having heard our family story, I understand why. Still, it's not fair to Ross. He's not responsible for the sins of her father.

"You're right," I say, a bit humbled. "I'm sorry."

Ross's face relaxes. I slide the first tape into the slot, hit Play, and settle in for a little male bonding.

There's a long silence, then shrill slasher music begins, a rip-off of Bernard Hermann's soundtrack for *Psycho*. Drum beats. Music swells. And a deep male voice begins: "There was a curse of death about Seymore Island . . . a curse proven by the graves of men who set foot on the forbidding shore, never to leave."

"Oh, thank goodness," I say. "I was afraid it might be melodramatic."

"*Zȷ̧-ȷ̧ȷ̧t!*" Ross hisses.

The deep male voice tells us that Seymore Island is now "crawling with accountants, attorneys, plumbers, housewives, and retired senior citizens who showed up on luxurious pleasure ships to gawk at their gravestones and ogle the comic penguins that inhabited a piece of the shoreline. Perhaps, just perhaps, the island would lay its curse on these intruders, too."

"Perhaps," Ross says.

"Just perhaps," I agree.

Enter the heroine, Maeve Fletcher: "Energetic and in constant motion, she moved about with a concentrated briskness and alive body."

"Alive body," I snicker. *Hoo boy, here we go . . .*

"She stared through eyes as blue as the deep sea from a strong face with high cheekbones. Her lips always seemed parted in a warm smile, revealing a tiny gap in the center of her upper teeth."

"I had a gap when I was a girl—"

"*Zȷ̧-ȷ̧ȷ̧t!*" Ross repeats.

"Maeve was three years shy of thirty with a master's degree in zoology."

We both burst out laughing—the first big laugh we've had together since the guy called for Clara.

Ross smiles. "See? I told you you'd like it."

To the west, toward New Orleans and Texas, the sun slides down the sky as the story unfolds, a mysterious shock wave slaughtering thousands of innocent penguins and a boatload of tourists. Dirk Pitt makes his entrance, picking his way through the dead bodies on board. He finds Deirdre Dorset in the lounge, slumped beside the piano.

"Their eyes locked for a moment and then he dropped his stare slightly. From what he could tell about her in her curled position, she had a fashion model's figure."

We crack up again, quieting back down as Dirk Pitt walks to the bar, grabs the Jack Daniels, and pours Deirdre a shot.

"After she gasped a few breaths of air, she looked into his sensitive green eyes and sensed his compassion."

"Ross," I say.

He slides his Oakleys down on his nose and looks at me, eyebrows raised. I look into his sensitive green eyes and sense his compassion. "Yeah," he says, "getting sappy. But before this trip's over, you're gonna hear the whole thing."

He pops out the tape, and the radio kicks in playing some hellfire preaching as we pass a handmade sign nailed to a pine tree: LITTER AND YOU BURN IN HELL.

He laughs, "You gotta love that upbeat religion."

He hits the Scan button. *Madame Butterfly*. I light up but he shoots me a look—*not just no but hell no*.

I hit Scan. A male voice is crooning "The Last Kiss."

I start to hit Scan again, but Ross says, "I *love* that song, Mom."

"A moldy oldie?"

"It's got the happiest beat but it's so *depressing*. I mean, come on, 'The Last Kiss'? I love the contrast."

I never thought about it quite that way. "I like it, too. I'm just a bit . . . superstitious." I wave my hand at the open road up ahead.

"*Puh!*" Ross says. "Superstitious." He starts singing along.

What the hell, I think, and join in for the chorus.

Oldies blaring, we drive through west Florida, crossing one river after another—Ochlockonee, Apalachicola, Chipola, Choctawhatchee—their names like some strange incantation, or perhaps, just perhaps, on this Easter weekend, a prayer for renewal.

By the time we cross the Blackwater River, Ross looks a bit brain-buzzed. He's been driving for almost three hours.

"You okay?"

"Yeah, fine," he says, but a few moments later he nods, jerks awake, and stares hard at the road.

"Tired?"

He shrugs. "A little."

It's almost six and I feel tired, too, but we have to make New Orleans tonight. We stop at McDonald's. I buy a large coffee. Ross orders two small burgers, extra pickles, no mustard.

He grins. "To tide me over till dinner."

The woman behind us in line notices the two Band-Aids on Ross's right knee, the result of a layout in Ultimate. "If you have girls, you don't have to go through all them bangs and bruises you do with boys."

I look at the woman's pale pockmarked face, then at Ross, and I flash back to him flying eighty-five miles an hour right behind the baby-blue semi—*See, Mom? We're drafting!* I sigh and smile at the woman. "You said a mouthful there, sister."

Back on the road, in the passenger seat, Ross bolts the burgers, wads the wrappers, and tosses them over his shoulder. "Catch you later." He throws back his seat and closes his eyes. Zonked. "Zonked out," as my dad used to say. "Zonko P. Boyo," I call Ross affectionately when he's exhausted. He takes on too much, doesn't get enough sleep—no wonder he's burned out—but if I suggest he do less, he just scowls and says, "I live a full life, Mom."

I adjust the side mirrors. Ross is sound asleep now, his long body folded to fit the small seat. *Like a fetus*, I think. The last month I was pregnant with him, my belly stuck out like a shelf. If I set my coffee cup there, Ross would throw a knee or elbow and slosh it. Now he's sleeping, dreaming, perhaps. A frown crosses his face.

I'm loved everywhere but my school.

What in the world did he mean? I look at him—a puzzle, a foreign country, a guy—and I wonder what's changed. I wonder if I'll ever know.

He shifts, leaning against the passenger window. I lock the passenger door so he doesn't fall out. The low sun lights his head, transforming his dark hair to gold.

I reach over and straighten a few stray strands of hair.

April 10, 1998, Good Friday

Trip budget: **$705.57**

McDonald's: −$3.04 (cash)

Balance remaining: **$702.53**

CHAPTER FOUR

Pensacola

The hills begin to give way to the coastal flatlands of West Florida, the oaks and pines giving way to Florida scrub and palmetto.

Ross is still sleeping, his breathing even and deep. I know he'll sleep a good while, so I click off the oldies. The late afternoon sky is as blue as Maeve Fletcher's eyes, the roadside still a bright Easter green. The gray pavement ahead has two darker grooves in the heavily trafficked right lane, but the newer stretches look more like gray suede, suede with sparkles, the sun catching bits of glass— mica?—mixed in the asphalt.

This is what I love about travel—how it heightens my senses. Some say travel is a vanishing act, disappearing down a rabbit hole, but for me it's appearing, coming into awareness. I look harder, see better. Time seems to slow down, expand.

Not long ago, I heard a report on NPR about time, why it seems to fly by the older we get. One expert chalked it up to routine. Time flows fast through the grooves that we've cut in our lives, like water rushing down a steep hillside. The antidote, he said, is breaking routines, doing spontaneous out-of-the-blue things.

Like this road trip. Yes, it's escape—Ross and I mean it as such—but it's also engagement, living full in the moment, paying attention as the journey unfolds. That's the secret—to let it unfold—not that we have any choice in the matter.

"A trip," Steinbeck says, "has personality, temperament, individuality, uniqueness . . . And all plans, safeguards, policing, and coercion are fruitless. We find after years of struggle that we do not take a trip; a trip takes us."

In other words, writes itself. A good thing, since I've given up writing.

An F-16 flies loud and low across Interstate 10. I notice a sign:

PENSACOLA
CRADLE OF NAVAL AVIATION

My first cradle. I was born in Ft. Lauderdale in 1951. Two weeks later, we moved to this Naval Air Station. My father was a flight instructor. We lived here until I was four. And I remember the jets. I *hated* the jets, the way they screamed over our quarters. I'd be playing peacefully out in the sand when I'd hear the jets coming and frantically try to gather my toys before the goddamn jets got there, but they were so fast I'd fling my toys in the air and run for the house.

I realize now, driving past Pensacola, that Interstate 10 connects my first home to my mother's and Ross's. Mom was born and raised in San Antonio. Ross was born in Jacksonville—where I-10 begins—and raised in three towns along I-10—Lake City, Live Oak, and now Tallahassee.

All things in our lives merge into one and I-10 runs through it.

And things come full circle. In 1995, when my father knew he was dying, he said he wanted to be buried here at the Barancas

National Cemetery. "I was happy in Pensacola," he told me. On December 15, we buried his ashes with full military honors. At his funeral, I read a piece from his *mémoire de l'air*, as he liked to call it, his account of flying into Hurricane Inga in 1961:

> We got off early and flew out into the Gulf and found Inga. In keeping with standard procedure, we flew into the "wall" of the hurricane at 500 feet, taking all the usual meteorological measurements, a rather bumpy trip with surface winds about 125 knots. The sea below was unbelievably rough, going in all directions, spume flying through the air. Finally we popped into the bright sunlight and calm air of the "eye." As we flew around in the eye, we were amazed to find that we were killing small birds on the windshield, apparently ones that had been trapped in the eye when it passed over land in Yucatan. We stuck around in the eye long enough to have a nice lunch, then we flew back into the wall in various directions to take measurements and finally climbed to 10,000 feet and exited at that altitude.

Of all the stories my father told, this one summed up how he lived. "On to the next great adventure," he'd say, and, finally, I think that's how he thought about dying. "Gone west," as his fellow aviators, the Quiet Birdmen, would say. And when Dad's memorial service ended with taps and a twenty-one-gun salute, a fellow QB flew over in Dad's favorite airplane—a Stearman—and tipped its wings back and forth in farewell.

Crossing the long bridge over Escambia Bay, looking out across the blue Gulf, I'm flooded again by feelings of loss. So many people I love slipping away—Dad, Mom, Anne, and now Ross. I feel a familiar lump in my throat. Since my parents divorced and Dad moved away, abandonment has been my big issue, my baggage deluxe.

I was five. We'd moved from Pensacola up to DC. Dad sat me on his lap in our den in Bethesda and said he was leaving. He wasn't going to live with us anymore. He was going to live with a woman named Joan who had a two-year-old, Dougie. After Dad left, I wandered out of the den—"Tears big as horse turds," my mother said—and I told her, very matter of fact, "Well, now Dougie has a daddy and we don't."

I went to see my father each summer, but leaving him was so painful I can still feel the cold airplane window against my hot face as I bawled my eyes out after saying goodbye.

The bridge comes to an end, and I pass a couple of slow-moving cars. The border between Alabama and Florida isn't too far ahead.

My parents divorced in DC, but Mom told me that the marriage was beginning to ravel in Pensacola. She recounted some happy times there:

It fulfilled a dream your father had to live in quarters overlooking a parade ground. Ours did. The parade ground in front of the Navy Photo School. That was paradise for you kids. I'd look out and you'd be dancing around in the ranks while the soldiers were marching. Or you'd be out there in your training pants panhandling from them. One time you brought home a quarter. You thought you were rich! It was heaven on earth, I mean, it really was. We'd go out and dance in the evening. Woody worked at Building 16, a psychology lab. He had wonderful colleagues who loved to come over.

But she also remembered hot summer evenings, my father stripped down to a T-shirt and skivvies, drinking his umpteenth beer and shouting at her, "You will not have an opinion in this house that isn't mine!"

"Well, I've got them!" she shouted back. "What are you going to do about that?"

I know when my father was young, he said some pigheaded things he regretted when he was old. I know he loved his beer. In Pensacola, he brewed his own in our bathtub, bottled it and gave it a name—Barancas Beer—until a chemist friend warned him that it could be lethal. From then on he bought "soldier beer"—3.2 percent alcohol—at the PX. The day I knew my father was dying was the day he didn't like beer anymore. But—vintage Johnson—he was damn funny about it, describing his decline in a letter to me:

As of Wednesday last I have suffered somewhat of a setback with sharp pains emanating from the area where I believe one's liver is supposed to be, extreme fatigue, and a further diminution of taste for beer*

His asterisk referred to a headline from the business section of the *Miami Herald* he'd taped at the end of the letter:

*COORS PROFITS DROP 37%.

But I didn't know until I interviewed my mother that the marital fault line could be traced back to Texas, to a death threat Granddaddy sent to my father—another death threat from those you think will protect you!—when my mother was pregnant with my sister, Patty. Mom was only nineteen, a year older than Ross will be—barely—when he leaves home at the end of next year.

I look at Ross, still sleeping beside me, and I realize that he doesn't know any of this. He's heard a few of my wild tomboy tales, but he's never heard the whole story. Not that any family story is whole. We're given pieces, like pottery shards. And it strikes me, crossing the Perdido River—remembering from my schoolgirl Spanish that *perdido* means "lost"—with my father gone and my mother's memory going, if I don't tell Ross the pieces I know, they'll be lost, too.

CHAPTER FIVE

Mobile

I tell Ross the story when we stop for dinner at a Subway just west of Mobile. The restaurant feels like a time capsule of the twentieth century—the walls covered with historic newspapers reproduced on bright yellow paper. The Beach Boys play on a juke box: "Surfin' USA," "Help Me Rhonda."

Ross sets down his meatball sandwich. "Your grandfather said that in a letter: 'If you weren't Patty Liz's father, you would be dead'?"

I nod, biting into my veggie special.

Ross tosses his napkin on the table. "Your granddad sent my granddad a death threat!"

"And you thought Clive Cussler was thrilling."

Ross is rapt. "Why'd he do it?"

"I asked Mom the same question." I tell Ross what she said.

He had no reason except he was so full of self-hatred he hated everyone else. He was so psychotic. You couldn't find any logical reason for what he did. He was a horrible pitiful alcoholic. And so cruel to your father. In 1947, they cut back the military, cashiered out anyone who wasn't regular Navy. The war was over. They didn't need them. Your father was heartbroken. Destroyed. He was just—what do I do? That's all he lived for, to be in the military. He was raised in the military, sent to military schools as a boy. And he had no place to go. But my father called him up and said he had a job down in Corpus. "You're gonna come work for me." Your father had a couple of years of engineering at Norwich, so he took the job. But the day he walked in the shop, my father treated him like the scum of the earth. A smart college boy. He hated him. We lived through hell, the things he did to your father. He wouldn't talk about it, but you could tell. When you have no pride left, you're not gonna brag about it. Then, just before your sister was born, Dad fired your father—his own son-in-law! Your father had to start his life all over again. He decided to go back to school, up in Houston, get a master's degree in psychology. I was pregnant with Patty. So we moved up to Houston, and Dad wrote him the letter: "If you weren't Patty Liz's father, you would be dead." We were on our way to Houston, and that was his parting shot. Your father was scared to death of him. Who wouldn't be? And he took the letter to a lawyer to see what charges he could press, if necessary, but my mother said, "Oh, my God, don't. He'll kill us all."

Ross's two thick eyebrows merge into one. "That's awful."

"But when Granddaddy was sober, it was a totally different story. He was a true genius—like you and Anne—and a brilliant engineer, self-taught. In 1951, when I was a baby, he revolutionized the shrimp industry, right here in Mobile."

"How?" Ross asks, clearly dazzled. I tell him what my mother told me:

> He built the refrigeration systems for the commercial fishermen. They usually got the shrimp and then iced them down. But then you'd have shrimp in a cake of ice and have to chip them out. Dad put this system in—designed it himself—so when the shrimp came out of the water, they were immediately frozen individually with very fine mist and very, very cold air. So you didn't have shrimp in a cake of ice and have to chip them out. Dad's were loose. And you'll see it in stores. He invented the process.

Ross is amazed. "Did he patent it?"

"Don't I wish! If he had, we wouldn't be taking this trip on a shoestring. But at least he and Mamaw enjoyed their time in Mobile."

> One day Dad said to Mother, "Let's go over and see the kids." So they drove over to Pensacola. Surprised us. But it was one of the nicest few days because Dad was being so good. He was busy. He was intelligent, inventive. We had a great time, and he was perfectly normal. I mean, he would do this, but the moments are golden because they're so few.

Ross guesses what's coming. "But all that changed when he drank."

"Yes, everything changed when he started drinking. Mom said his eyes would get this murderous look—"

"Dr. Jekyll and Mr. Hyde."

"Mom's words exactly. It's heartbreaking, really. He drank to drown his self-hatred, but it just made it worse, so he took it out on others, especially Mamaw. He'd insult her, slap her around."

Ross winces.

"Mom said there were times he beat her beyond recognition."

Ross stares at his meatball sandwich.

"Sorry," I say. "Not exactly dinnertime conversation. And probably something you don't need to know."

"I *do*, Mom," he says passionately. "It's our family history. I need to know."

I cock my head, reappraising—I had no idea Ross has such a passion for family. I think of Mary Pipher's wisdom in *The Shelter of Each Other*: "To be strong the family must build walls that give the family definition, identity and power." One way she recommends is sharing family stories. And my dearest wish is to rebuild our crumbling family wall. So I continue. "Mamaw tried to leave him, divorcing him twice, but he threatened to kill her if she didn't come back. She was scared. She felt helpless. A classic battered woman. So she did."

Ross chews slowly, taking this in. "And he threatened to kill your father, too."

"Yes," I say. "The sad thing was, my father blamed my mother for that."

"Is that why your parents divorced?"

"It wasn't the only reason, but Mom said it was a factor."

He held that against me. It was one of the reasons we got divorced. But it wasn't my fault. I didn't know what to do. I was nineteen years old.

"Poor Mimaw," Ross says.

"They didn't divorce for another eight years, but she said one of the causes was that letter. Something my father couldn't forget."

"Or forgive."

"No. Not that Mom didn't harbor a grudge or two of her own."

"Like what?"

"Pigheaded things my dad said to her."

Ross frowns. "That goes for everyone, right?"

"What?"

"Saying pigheaded things."

"Absolutely," I say, remembering that Ross adored his grandfather. And vice versa. "My favorite grandson," Dad called him, a witty and safe compliment since his four other grandchildren were girls. "And I know Dad regretted some of the unkind things he said. That Mom couldn't cope with his faculty friends. That she was stupid. That she'd never give up anything for an education."

Ross smiles, knowing what she became, but he has no idea what she went through to get there.

"The marriage finally fell apart after we moved to DC and Dad left us for Joan and her two-year-old, Dougie.

"Uncle Doug," Ross says, connecting the dots.

"I loved Doug—and still do—but I didn't understand why Dad left us. Since no one talked about feelings in our family, I thought Dad left because of something I'd done."

"Geez, Mom," Ross says.

"I felt so guilty. Lost. And *ashamed*. Because *no one's* parents were divorced in those days. And I think Mom felt lost, too. I know she was worried sick about money. Dad sent us three hundred dollars a month, but rent in Bethesda took half. Mom started working part-time, selling shoes at a department store—Fedway—but she hated it. She tried real estate but hated that more. So she quit and took her first college class at American U. Political science. She said her hand was shaking so badly the first day of class she could barely take notes. But she loved it."

"Her bliss."

"Yes. And she made an A."

Ross looks at me—*so?*—because everyone makes A's in our family.

"All her life, her father—and mine—told her she was stupid. This professor told her she wasn't. He said she should go to college full-time, and she wanted to, badly, but she couldn't afford it. We couldn't even afford to stay in Bethesda. The summer after I finished first grade, we moved to these depressing apartments in Silver Spring—stark, redbrick two-story buildings. Bleak. A real moonscape. Trains roared past day and night."

"Sounds like the projects."

"It may have been. I didn't know a soul in the place, so I'd hang out by the tracks, putting pennies down on the rails."

Ross blinks. "You did that, too?"

I blanch. "Did *you* do it?"

He shrugs. "Maybe. A few times."

"You could've been killed!"

"So could you!"

"That's different!"

He raises an eyebrow.

"Okay, my mother would've *croaked* if she'd known. I was only six, maybe seven. This skinny little girl. I remember the force of the train roaring by slamming me into the brick wall, but I'd still do it. Wait for the train to pass, then pick up my penny. I loved how it looked—all bent and wavy, like the melting clock in that painting by Salvador Dali."

"*The Persistence of Memory*."

"Ah," I say, surprised that he knows this. "It's strange what persists. What we remember. Why putting pennies down on the tracks?"

"You were lonely," Ross says.

I feel a rush of love for this boy, for his understanding, compassion. And mine deepens for him as I realize he must feel lonely, too.

"I *was* lonely," I say. "All summer. Then Mamaw and Granddaddy flew out to see us. Granddaddy took Patty and me to our favorite toy store in Bethesda—Loretta's—and let each of us pick out a toy.

Ross smiles. "What did you pick?"

"Davy Crockett outfits. Fringed leather vests and fake raccoon caps."

"No raccoons were harmed in the making of these outfits."

"We thought we were the nuts, strutting around like you wouldn't believe."

Ross leans back, grinning. "Yes, I would."

"We had a good time with Granddaddy."

"Because he was sober."

"The strange thing was that *Mamaw* seemed drunk. They stayed a couple of weeks, and the whole time she stayed in bed in her long blue nightgown. Which wasn't like her at all. She always prided herself on being a lady. And she was—a real beauty. Always dressed up just so." I spare Ross the details but I can still see her— slender and tall like my mother, in a crisp shirtwaist dress with a jacket and felt hat to match. "Mom was afraid that Mamaw was having some kind of breakdown, and she wanted to help, so she decided to move back to Texas. It was cheaper to live there, and Patty and I would be around family—our Aunt Patty and her boys, Jeff and Jon. So Patty and I flew back to Corpus with Mamaw and Granddaddy while Mom packed our stuff."

"She wasn't worried about sending you with them?"

"She knew they'd be on their best behavior with us. And they were. I remember sitting next to Granddaddy on the airplane, fascinated by the hair on his arm."

Ross laughs.

"I know it sounds crazy, but I loved how it looked—like spun gold. I sat there stroking his arm so the golden hairs would all lie one direction, like grass in the wind. Wouldn't that drive you nuts, having some little kid do that?"

"Big time," Ross says.

"But he didn't mind. Maybe he knew I was lonely. Maybe he was lonely, too." I look across the table at Ross, hoping he'll open up, but he's studying the inside of his bag of chips. His eyelashes are thick, dark, and shiny, like mink. He throws back his head and dumps the last potato chip crumbs in his mouth.

"And that, my dear boy, is how I got to Texas." I finish my veggie sub and wad up the paper. Ross looks me in the eye—*Oh, yeah? Watch this!* He crushes his potato chip bag. I laugh. We toss our trash in a bin that says THANK YOU!

Outside, the air is sweet balmy perfection. To the west, toward Texas, a lingering twilight. To the east, toward Tallahassee, a full moon rising. Ross and I squeeze in the Mystique. I drive. He pops in *Shock Wave*. And we listen all the way to New Orleans.

April 10, 1998, Good Friday

Trip budget: **$702.53**

Subway: −$5.86 (cash)
Gas: −$10.73 (Visa)

Balance remaining: **$685.94**

CHAPTER SIX

New Orleans

My mother and sister and I lived in Corpus Christi for three years before we moved to Kingsville and I met Ann Owens, but that's a piece of the story I'll tell Ross later. We're approaching New Orleans now, the bright lights of the city off in the distance beyond the dark expanse of Lake Pontchartrain. The full moon is shining over the Gulf.

Ross pops out the Cussler tape we just finished and tosses it in the back seat. "I can't believe I've never met Ann."

"Me, either." I've talked about her all his life. When he was little, at bedtime, I'd tell him about our wild tomboy time, a female Huck Finn and Tom Sawyer childhood immortalized in a black-and-white poster-sized photo framed on our dining room wall— Ann and I, twelve at most, her arm slung over my shoulder, the two of us wearing bathing suits, grinning into the camera, our hair, faces, bodies *slathered* with mud.

But since Ann and I grew up and started our careers and our families, we've been so busy our paths seldom cross, even though we only live a six-hour drive apart. I met her first three children on a previous visit, but I still haven't met her fourth child, my godson Scott, now six years old.

"Meeting Ann will be like meeting a *legend*," Ross says.

I laugh. "She'll love that." I wonder if Scott will feel the same way.

We drive across a section of Lake Pontchartrain, the headlights of oncoming cars strobing in the guardrail between us, then we follow I-10 as it shoots through New Orleans. The city where my mother and father spent their honeymoon. The city founded 180 years ago, almost to the day, by Jean-Baptiste Le Moyne, Sieur de Bienville, on what he called "one of the most beautiful crescents" on the Mississippi River. Which we can see on the right. The port of New Orleans is off to the left.

We pass a sign for Elysian Fields.

"Elysian Fields is a big deal in *A Streetcar Named Desire*," I tell Ross.

"Mmm," he says, underwhelmed. "It also means 'paradise.'"

"Does it?"

"In mythology, yeah." He's been competing this year in Certamon—brain bowl competitions in Latin.

We hurtle on through the city.

Ross lights up, pointing. "The Superdome!" His subtext is clear—*There's drama and then there's* great *drama*.

"Designed by Ann's husband Greg's sister-in-law's father," I say, then laugh. "As if anyone could process all that."

Ross grabs the guidebook and flips on the Mystique's dome light, which doesn't help my lousy night vision. "Wow," he says, reading aloud. "'Twenty-seven stories high. Covers 9.7 acres. Cost $163 million dollars to build, almost *eleven times* what the United States paid for the Louisiana Purchase.'"

"Thank you for that barrage of statistics," I smile, clicking off the dome light. "Help me watch for our exit."

Too late. We sail over a rise and there's a fork in I-10, the signs coming at us too fast to sort out: SLIDELL, BATON ROUGE.

I panic. "Which one?" I shout.

"I don't know!" Ross shouts back.

I veer right, but it's wrong. We take a curve around a poorly lit highway cloverleaf, centrifugal force throwing us dangerously close to a low concrete wall, much too low to stop the Mystique if I were to hit it. I don't, but I'm terrifyingly close, nearly scraping Ross's passenger door as I think, *Scrape the wall and this road trip is over.* The road narrows, barely wide enough for one car, then straightens out and starts up a sharp incline that seems to disappear into the darkness. The *batick batick batick* of the tires reminds me of the *click click click* of Kumba and Montu at Busch Gardens, as Ross and I go up up up up, approaching what I'm guessing will be a sickening plunge. My heart goes *squish squish* again.

"Damn, damn, damn, *damn!*"

"Easy, Mom, chill."

Sure enough, the road plummets. We careen—almost carom—around another tight curve, graffiti flashing in my peripheral vision—*Graffiti! Who the hell would climb up here?*—as the road corkscrews down and around to a dingy part of the city—gas stations and pawnshops and boarded-up buildings. *The Boulevard of Broken Dreams.*

"You sure you meant to go this way, Mom?"

"Ha ha," I say. "Lock your door." I stop at a red light.

Ross points to a half-dozen tough-looking guys about his own age slouched against a brick wall. "Why don't you ask them directions?"

"Oh, right." Is he *crazy?*

"Then I'll ask them."

"Not on your life."

"People are basically good, Mom."

"I agree. I just want you to live to see Texas."

"*Puh!*" he says. He shoots me that look again—*wimp!*

"Think what you want. I think you're too trusting."

"I think you're a racist."

I flash, "*I'm not a racist!*"

The light changes. I floor it. Our wheels spin on wet pavement then grab. The Mystique fishtails—straightens—and lurches ahead.

"Smooth move, Ex-Lax."

I take a deep breath. Before we left Tallahassee, I promised myself I would not have a meltdown.

"And you know I'm not a racist. I've spent the last seven years of my life bulldogging the story of Ruby McCollum—and finally cracked it."

"Then you quit."

I'm tempted again to tell him about the death threat from the Klan, but this doesn't feel like the right time or place, so I let it go.

Up ahead, on the corner, there's a brand-new gas station lit up like the Death Star. An African-American woman dressed to the nines—red-leather coat with a leopard-skin collar and four-inch spiked heels—is filling her tank.

I pull up beside her and roll down my window and say, a bit sheepish, "Could you tell me how to get back to Interstate 10?"

Her smile is warm but indulgent—*silly honky.* "That's easy— next light, turn right. It'll drop you right back on I-10."

"Thanks so much," I say, grateful. I crank up my window and

my best Blanche DuBois accent for Ross. "I have always relied on the kindness of strangers."

I wait for his groan.

"Okay," he says, "you're not a racist. A quitter, yes, but not a racist."

"Thank you."

"You know what you are?"

"What?" I brace for an insult.

"You're cool, Mom."

Now I do a whiplash double take—*me?*

"Momzilla," he adds.

"Momzilla." I chuckle and savor the compliment (I'm pretty sure it's a compliment) all the way to Ann's beautiful three-story home just west of New Orleans in Metairie where she and her children welcome us warmly.

"You met in a laundromat, right?" Ross leans forward in his Star Wars T-shirt.

Ann laughs, "Oh, Lord."

We've settled into her family room overlooking a moonlit walled garden, Ross and I and Ann and her four children—Lauren, twelve; Elizabeth, ten; Gregory, Jr., eight; and Scott, six, who nestles beside me on the soft gray leather couch. Ann sits on the opposite end, flanked by the girls. Ross and Greg Jr. sprawl in big easy chairs.

"Godmother," Scott murmurs, patting my arm.

I can't help smiling at that. It feels like a gift—Scott coming into my life as Ross is leaving. *The Law of Conservation of Connection*, I muse. *Human nature abhors an emotional vacuum.*

Scott pulls the quilt over his silky blond hair and leans into me.

I hear the muted *tink tink tinky tink* of the Florida State fight song played by the wind-up musical FSU stuffed bear that I brought him. By the time the fight song winds down, he's fast asleep.

"Yep, a laundromat," I tell Ross, Greg Jr., Elizabeth, and Lauren. "I pulled this big canvas cart out from under the table where you folded your laundry, and there was this person curled up inside. Scared the pee out of me."

"The peewaddle," Ann corrects me. Our favorite expression when we were ten.

"It was like seeing myself in the mirror—the same freckles and cap cut."

"And sense of humor," she says.

"Ann hopped out of the cart, and we both stood there laughing."

"Howling."

"Which pretty well set the tone."

"Instant soul mates," Ann says. "I invited your mother back to my house, and we climbed the mesquite tree in the backyard."

"Bared our souls," I added.

"Discovered we had so much in common."

"Like what?" Lauren asks.

I smile at Ann. "Tomboys."

She smiles back. "Bright."

"Funny."

"And humble," Ross says.

We laugh.

"Our mothers were both academics. Divorced. Single mothers." I look at Ross. "The day I met Ann, the shame I felt about my parents' divorce went away."

"Mine, too," Ann says.

Ross looks at us. "Wow."

"We sat in Ann's mesquite tree and told each other what we wanted to be."

Ann nods. "I said a doctor. Your mom said a writer."

"And that's what you *are*," Elizabeth says with true amazement.

Ross cuts me a look—*quitter!*—but I'm saved by Ann's husband, Greg, coming home, still on call, in his white cardiologist jacket.

"Welcome," he says in his soft N'Orleans accent. "Good to see you again." He busses my cheek.

I introduce him to Ross, who unfolds from the armchair and stands a few inches taller than Greg. They shake hands, and Greg sinks, exhausted, into an empty chair.

It's eleven o'clock, Florida time, but only ten here, so we stay up and talk for a while. Most nights I'd be as zonked out as Scott by this hour, but Ann keeps me laughing, as she always has, regaling Ross and her kids with the practical jokes we perpetrated on the unsuspecting residents of Kingsville, Texas. "Our specialty was stuffing old clothes and laying them by the curb so they looked like dead bodies."

"*Mom.*" Lauren laughs.

"Then we'd hide in the bushes," her mother continues.

"Oh, yeah," I say. "We loved watching drivers slam on their brakes."

"Motorcycles fishtail to a stop."

"But our masterpiece—" I crack up laughing.

"Our *masterpiece*—" Ann cracks up, too.

"—was playing this hit 45 that Ann had."

Ross and the other children look blank.

"A single on vinyl."

They nod.

I remember the single. "They're Coming to Take Me Away—'"

"—Ha-Haaa!" Ann and I shout together and laugh.

Ross laughs, too, though more at us, I suspect, than the story. He's heard it before, but never this way, with stereo mothers.

"Wait, no," Ann says. "That wasn't the single. It was the one with machine-gun fire."

"Right. Followed by screaming and sirens."

"And a police bullhorn booming, 'PULL OVER! PULL OVER!'"

"God," I laugh. "I'd forgotten 'PULL OVER.'"

We can't remember that single's title, but we can remember what we did with its sound effects.

"We spent hours practicing dropping the phonograph needle—"

"Until we could hit the precise sound effect that we wanted."

The children's faces move back and forth with our banter, like courtside spectators at a tennis match.

Ann looks at Ross. "We dragged my portable record player out to the bushes by the street in back of my house."

"What, five or six extension cords?"

"Easy."

"And we waited there in the bushes until someone walked by."

"Some poor, unsuspecting, innocent soul."

"Then we saw Jerome Staggers."

Ann shakes her head. "Poor buck-toothed Jerome."

"An overbite like a back hoe."

"Just strolling by, enjoying the evening."

"*Tra la la, tra la la.*"

"And we dropped the needle on the machine gun fire."

"BLAM BLAM BLAM BLAM!"

"And watched Jerome rise into the air."

We howl. So does Ross. Lauren, Elizabeth, and Greg Jr. laugh with us, too, amazed that their mother—Dr. Ann Tilton, head of pediatric neurology at LSU—was such a rascal.

"Poor Jerome," Ann says.

"We were awful."

"Terrible."

"Wicked."

We crack up laughing again.

I glance at Greg, the ghost of a smile on his pale tired face, and I hope he doesn't think I'm corrupting his children. "It was a safer world then," I remind them.

Ross laughs. "Not for Jerome!"

"No." Ann pulls a serious face for her children. "Do not try this at home."

"Or at camp," Ross adds. "Last summer at Duke, I got busted."

News to me. "Busted for what?"

He grins. "Shooting Skittles."

Greg Jr. and his sisters light up—he's talking their language!

He explains. "I was hanging out with my friends, Dan and Dave, at the Duke TIP summer program, goofing off in Dave's closet, and I got stuck inside. Okay, they locked me in. And I found this lead pipe, a hollow one you hang clothes on. They let me out, and we started playing with it. Dave had this drawer full of Skittles, and we're like, "Hey, we could shoot some people out on the Quad.""

Greg Jr. leaps up from his chair. "BLAM BLAM BLAM BLAM!"

"Calm down," his father says softly.

Ann warns, "Do *not* try this at home."

"So we took the screen off the dorm window and started pelting these kids walking by. There were thirteen of us standing on Dave's bed, laughing our asses—"

He catches the look on my face—*language*!

"—cracking up at all the people getting pelted with Skittles, until we hit a counselor. Who looked up and saw us. So Dave shouts, 'We're busted!' We all ran away, but the counselor knew we'd been in Dave's room. So he calls Dave into his office and tells him he has to say who was there. Dave refuses to rat his friends out. The counselor gives him until the next day to come up with the list or he's sending Dave home. Next morning we're out on the Quad, and Dave's feeling screwed because his parents will freak if Duke sends him home early, but he won't name names. I tell him he can use mine, and he's like, 'Wait! Let's ask everyone who shot Skittles to sign a petition. Everyone who *saw* us shoot Skittles. They can't send us *all* home.' We got four lists going, getting more and more people to sign it."

"I'm Spartacus," I say, laughing. What else can I do?

"I'm Spartacus," Ann chimes in.

"Yeah," Ross laughs, "exactly. By the end of the day, when we had to go face the music, we handed the counselor this petition with all these names, and he's like, 'What the hell is this?'"

Ann's kids titter.

"And Dave said, 'You asked me to name names. These are all the people involved.' And the counselor just started laughing. Then the on-site coordinator came in, and the counselor showed him the list, and the coordinator looked at us and said, 'Could you circle the main ones?'"

Ann and Greg and I laugh with Ross. The joke's a bit lost on the kids, but I can tell by their faces they think Ross is cool. The essence of cool.

"You're a rascal," Ann tells him. High praise. "A chip off the old block."

Ross is still laughing so hard at the Skittles story he falls back in his chair, his face contorted with laughter. The way my dad used to laugh. The way Ann and I laughed in the laundromat the first day we met. The way Ross must have laughed with Dan and Dave up at Duke. They were all he talked about when he got home last summer—Dan and Dave and Ultimate Frisbee. And it strikes me now that maybe they're the reason he wants to graduate early. He's their age, but because of his late August birthday, he's a year behind them in school. If he left Maclay a year early, he could start college when they do.

Greg slaps his knees, stands up, says goodnight. "If I don't sleep now, I won't sleep at all." He kisses Ann and their children. "I'm glad you're here," he tells Ross and me, then he heads off to bed.

It's midnight—one in the morning, Florida time—so we call it a night. I scoop Scott up in his quilt and carry him and his FSU *tinky-tink* bear up the stairs to his bedroom. The other kids follow.

"Who's Spartacus?" Greg Jr. says.

CHAPTER SEVEN

New Orleans

The phone by my bed rings at five in the morning—one ring, then it stops. Greg, still on call, must have picked up. Somewhere in this city, someone's heart has stopped beating.

I lie under the drifts of white comforter in the upstairs guest room and listen to my own heart. I think of my father, how blissful he looked when he died. The beatific smile on his face—*On to the next great adventure!* I think of Ross, how sad he's been this semester, how disconnected he seems from his friends at Maclay. "What friends?" he said. Have I done the right thing bringing him on this road trip? I think of my mother, who loved the idea, even though I told her the trip was a splurge and Ross and I would have to give up other things to afford it. "Kids don't need things, they need time," she said, her parenting credo since I was a child.

Out front, a car door slams. I hear Greg drive away. Day dawns in the dormer. I get out of bed and look out the window at another spectacular day—the powder-blue sky, the profusion of flowers—azaleas, begonias, Easter lilies—in Ann and Greg's landscaped gardens. It dawns on me it's the day before Easter. Easter Eve.

I walk down the hall and peek in Ann's room to see if she's awake. No, sound asleep. Lauren on one side, Elizabeth on the other. Scott and Greg Jr. curled up in a nest of quilts on the floor. "Nightcrawlers," Ann calls them. I round the corner to the boys' bedroom. Ross is sprawled across a twin bed, limbs flung at odd angles, deep in tangled teen sleep. He looks so far under I doubt a depth charge could wake him.

I close the door, close my eyes, make a wish—*I hope on this Easter weekend our relationship will resurrect, too.*

Where do you take five children, ages six to sixteen, in a city so rich in history, culture, cuisine? The Audubon Zoo!

Ann and I watch our five kids tear around the elephant fountain. She laughs at their antics. "Which is the zoo?"

I snap photos. Ross, Lauren, Greg Jr., Elizabeth, and Scott, striking poses in front of the fountain. Lining up to buy Roman candy. Taking turns riding a bronze Komodo dragon. An albino alligator that looks like it's made of white chocolate peering out from under a log. Ross helping Scott dig up faux artifacts at a faux Mayan dig. Carrying Scott piggyback with a sweet patient look on his face—*He ain't heavy, he's my godbrother.* And later, Ross glaring into the camera, impatient with me, the Momarazzi—*Enough with the pictures!*—a string of pink taffy hanging out of his mouth.

He snatches the camera.

"Easy!" I say.

He insists on taking a picture of Ann and me side by side, Ann's arm slung over my shoulder in a reprise of the mud photograph, then he passes the camera to Ann and sits beside me on a bench. He's sitting precisely the way that I'm sitting—right foot resting on the left knee.

So much alike, I think with pleasure, until I realize he's mimicking me. I force a grim smile for the camera, and Ross does the same, our faces shadowed by our baseball caps. A mother-and-son *American Gothic*.

"When they're the least lovable, that's when they need the most loving," Ann offers.

I shove Ross with my shoulder and wag my finger at him. "I *love* you, man."

"*Puh!*" He laughs, trapping me in a headlock.

Scott and Greg Jr. go wild and leap up on the bench.

"Dog pile on the rabbit!" I shout, another Kingsville expression. Lauren and Elizabeth pile on, too.

Ann snaps a picture.

Ross lightens up when we get to the primates, another one of his passions. He lifts Scott up on his shoulders. Ann and I lean on the rail, watching our children watch an orangutan watching the crowd. It spies a woman eating some chips and sticks out its hand, palm open—*Sister, can you spare a chip?* The woman's up on zoo rules and won't feed him. A minute passes—a stare-down between them. The orangutan sticks out its tongue. The crowd roars. Ross is lurching with laughter, the way he did when we went to Busch Gardens last year and watched a young chimp whack an old chimp with a stick. The old chimp chased the young chimp up a tree, snatched the stick, and broke it over its knee. *Commedia del ape.* Ross swore he'd study primates in college.

College. *Don't think about that.*

In a snit, the orangutan turns its back on the crowd. Ross and Scott laugh.

Ann smiles at me. "Ross is a wonderful kid."

"You think so?"

"There's such a warmth to him. A generosity."

I look at him, hugging Scott. "He's always had a great heart. Or did before he turned into a teen."

Ann laughs. "Well, my kids adore him."

"Yeah," I say, wistful. "Me, too."

We grab lunch at the zoo's own McDonald's and squeeze around a table outside. I peel the paper off a Big Mac. "Isn't fast food a sin in this city?"

"Absolutely," Ann says. "And I just had a brainstorm!" She pulls out her cell phone and calls her mother-in-law. "Could the boys stay with you while we go to dinner?" Scott and Greg Jr. overhear and start protesting loudly. "Hush," Ann says. "You're too young."

When she hangs up Ross asks, "Where are we going?"

Ann grins. "Galatoire's."

Gussied up a few hours later, we all head for the Quarter in Ann's white Suburban. She drops Scott and Greg, Jr. off with Greg's mother.

"See you later, man," Ross says, punching their shoulders. He's sitting behind us in a navy-blue jacket he borrowed from Greg, who's meeting us at the restaurant. Elizabeth and Lauren sit behind Ross—in the way back—in their best Easter dresses. A Renoir pastel.

Ann and I are still laughing about Jerome Staggers.

I fill Ross and the girls in. "We were making telescopes for Mr. Troutman in eighth grade science."

"A simple assignment," Ann adds. "Two lenses clipped to a yardstick."

"But Jerome was taking his own sweet time, and Mr. Troutman was getting a little—"

"PO'd," Ann says.

"So Jerome clipped on the lenses and aimed his yardstick telescope at Mr. Troutman's bald head and shouted, "There's life on the moon!""

When we finally stop laughing, Ross leans forward. "Do you know you two are the embodiment of Scout?"

I look at him. "*To Kill a Mockingbird* Scout?"

"Yes."

I lean toward Ann and say, confidential, "I think he's saying we haven't come all that far since we took the mud picture."

Ann slows down. "We could let him out here."

I laugh, "Pull over, pull over!"

"No!" Ross shouts. "I'm just saying . . . "

We look at him—*yes?*

"It's like you could entertain yourselves forever in a world all your own. Like you don't care what anyone thinks."

Ann and I look at each other and laugh brightly.

"See?" Ross says. "Just like Scout. 'Pass the damn ham.'"

We are walking along Bourbon Street. Blues and jazz waft out open doors in the soft evening air.

"The French Quarter was built by the Spanish," Ann says.

"Ah," I say. "So it's just a clever name."

Ann laughs. "The French built it first, but it burned down in two fires under the Spanish, so they're the ones who rebuilt it."

"Amazing." I look up at the bright-colored buildings, the balconies with their lacy wrought-iron grillwork. "Did you hear that?" I ask Ross.

He doesn't hear me. He's walking ahead of us between Lauren and Elizabeth, trying hard not to look at the photos of strippers plastered on windows. I feel a rush of sympathy for him, on that fragile cusp between boy and man. He walks under a hand-painted sign—LUST IS LIFE, THE REST IS JUST DETAILS—and shouts, relieved, "Galatoire's!"

Lauren looks back at Ann. "I'm sitting by Ross!"

Elizabeth shoves her. "No, *I* am!"

"Hey," Ann admonishes gently. "Ross has two sides."

Ross holds the door open for us. I go in last. He gives me a bittersweet smile. *Smiles with a charming sadness*, as Tennessee Williams once put it. "See?" Ross says. "I'm loved everywhere but my school."

We sit in bentwood chairs around a long table with a white tablecloth near the back of the ninety-year-old French Creole bistro, a narrow dining room brightly lit by brass chandeliers, the walls lined with white-framed mirror panels and polished brass coat hooks.

Greg has joined us, however briefly, and sits at the head of the table. Ross sits on his right, flanked by the girls. Ann and I sit at the opposite end of the table, in a world all our own, marveling at these beautiful children we hatched.

There's a budding sophistication to Ross I haven't noticed before. Here he is, right at home in this elegant restaurant. At ease, relaxed, in Greg's navy-blue blazer, sampling the filet that Greg recommended. When Ross tastes it, his eyelashes flutter.

"Lord," I whisper to Ann. "I hope he doesn't spill on Greg's jacket."

"Don't worry," she says. "I pulled one from the dry-cleaning pile."

We laugh.

Ann gazes at our kids. "Do you think our mothers did this?"

"What?"

"Marveled at us when we went out to eat."

"I hope so," I say.

"El Jardin," Ann remembers. Our mothers' favorite restaurant in Kingsville. Both were financially strapped single mothers, but they'd take us out when they could. "The best Tex-Mex in the world," Ann's mother, Harriette, used to say, and she loved food second only to Ann. When you returned from a trip, she didn't ask what you saw, she asked what you *ate*.

"I miss your mother," I say.

"Me, too." Ann's eyes glisten. Harriette died when my Anne was three. Colon cancer, just like my father. She never met her grandchildren.

"How's your mom?" Ann asks.

I fill her in on the watershed stroke, the garbled language, the carotid artery surgery, her gradual memory loss.

Ann nods. "That's consistent with left-hemisphere lesions."

"Her doctor thinks it's dementia, not Alzheimer's disease."

"That's a blessing."

"But I guess there's no real way of knowing."

"Not without an autopsy, no." She frowns, as if it's her fault that medical science is so imprecise. "It must be so hard. For her and for you."

"It is. But harder for her. Such fierce pride. And a *historian*, for God's sake."

"She was always so brilliant."

"Both our moms were. And brave."

Ann chuckles. "Imagine, raising us all alone."

"Two phoenixes rising up from the mud."

"Trying to educate us."

I paraphrase *A River Runs Through It*. "There was a fine line between education and religion in our family."

Ann laughs. "*No* line."

I wish Ross were hearing this, but the girls are telling him about their soccer teams.

"Lauren's might make it to state," Ann says proudly.

"You girls are triple threats," I suggest. "Athletic, beautiful, brainy."

They laugh, embarrassed, but clearly pleased.

"You'll be under all kinds of pressure to dumb down," I tell them. "People will say it's not cool to be smart. The same thing happened to Ross's sister."

"And me," Ross says.

"But don't you listen to them."

Lauren and Elizabeth nod.

Greg looks at his daughters. "Are you listening to Claudia, girls? You need to hear this." But they're listening to Ross tell them about Ultimate.

The waiter sets a plate of soft-shelled crabs in front of Greg. "Doctor," he says to Greg with a thick Hungarian accent. Then he waits, blushing with pleasure, as Greg tells Ross and me about the waiter's son and daughter—one at Yale, one at Stanford.

"I'm thinking about Stanford," Ross says.

"A good choice," the waiter says, bowing slightly. He returns to the kitchen as Greg's beeper beeps.

"Hospital," he says. "I have to get back." He kisses the girls, shakes Ross's hand, waves goodbye to us at the end of the table, and goes.

"Ultimate's *huge* at Stanford," Ross tells the girls. "One of the few places it's a varsity sport. There and Yale."

Ann looks confused. "What's Ultimate?"

"Ross's passion. His new sport. Well, that and pole vaulting."

Ann's face contorts, confirming my worst fears. "Don't *ever* tell a neurologist your child is pole vaulting!"

"That bad?"

"Oh, honey, you don't want to know."

I look down the table at Ross, still healthy and whole, explaining the intricacies of the game to Elizabeth and Lauren.

"Players line up in the center of the field. You play either as a thrower or first man in the stack."

Ann looks at me. "Thrower?"

"The player throwing the Frisbee." And that, I realize with a flash of self-anger, is about all I know—*about my son's bliss*! I've only been to one tournament, and I had a good time watching him play, but I had no idea what I was seeing. "Ross," I say, channeling Billy Crystal in *When Harry Met Sally*, "please to explain to Ann what Ultimate is."

He looks surprised and happy I asked. "It's like soccer played with a Frisbee, which we call the disc."

"Ah," Ann and I say together.

"Flatball, we call it. Seven players advancing the disc. You score when you hit your man in the end zone. Or woman," he says to the girls. "So it's sort of like football. In terms of possession, it's more like basketball—you've got ten seconds to pass or you turn it over. But one throwing motion, the hammer, is like serving in tennis, and the layouts are like sliding in baseball."

"Layouts?" Ann says, a bit lost.

"Swan dives for the disc," I say. At least I know that.

"But the coolest thing is the spirit of the game. Everyone's out there, see—" He's on fire. "Ultimate is designed for excitement and looking good. As a player. The whole point of Ultimate is really just to look good while you're doing it. Style. Throwing a Frisbee can be such a graceful art. And it's like everyone out there is trying to play their best, but they respect other people, like if you see an exciting play by an opponent, you're gonna go, 'Wow!' You're not gonna say, 'You suck!'"

The girls laugh.

"It's about respecting your opponent and being friends with them. It's definitely a brotherhood. And sisterhood," he adds quickly. "Since you're playing Ultimate, you're automatically initiated. The minute you touch the disc everyone out there is great to you. Even if you can't stand them off the field, when you get out there, there's nothing else. It's just the playing, and you're obviously competing, but it's not at the expense of—there's never an FSU-Florida football thing. There can be rivalries, but they're not insanely fierce or bitter. Everything stays on the field. No one's trying to get away with anything because they know it's out there. It's self-regulated. Officiated. You're not trying to get it past a ref. Fouls happen, but you work it out with the other players." He picks up his fork. "It's the way other sports used to be before they got big and corrupted by money."

An aria. I'm dazzled.

So is Ann. "Wow."

Does he blush?

"Ross," I say with real pride. "I knew you loved Ultimate, but I had no idea you connected on a philosophical level."

"Oh, yeah," he says. "I'm telling you, it's about love, respect, looking good, *grace*." He tastes the crab. His eyelashes flutter again.

Ann shakes her head, amazed. "I've never even *heard* of the sport."

"I hadn't either before I went to Duke's summer program," Ross says. "It's big there, but it's huge in the Ivies. Brown's the best."

I tell Ann it's one of the reasons Ross wants to graduate early.

"You want to graduate early?"

I can hear the concern in her voice.

So can Ross. He shoots me a look—*Oh, thanks a lot, Mom.* "Why don't you tell Ann what *you* quit?"

"Hey," I tell him, "pass the damn crab."

Later. We are sitting in Ann's Suburban on the southern shore of Lake Pontchartrain. The moon is up. Ross and Lauren and Elizabeth are down by the water, skipping flat rocks. They leap off the edge of the grass onto the narrow beach a few feet below so we'll think they've fallen into the water. We're amused but not fooled. Ross is so tall his back is showing. They look back at us—no reaction—and resume skipping rocks.

I look at the moon out over the lake. One of the moon's craters, I remember, is named Lake of Dreams. Ann is the trustee of the dream I once had of being a writer. I confided the dream first to her in the mesquite tree in her backyard, but I didn't begin to write until my mid-twenties, after she called and said she'd been accepted to UT Galveston's medical school. I still remember the electric jolt that I felt—*She's following her bliss and I'm not!* It was an alarm, a wake-up call. So I dropped out of graduate school, took a waitressing job, and started writing.

I glance at Ann, her face pale in the moonlight. Maybe because tomorrow is Easter or because Greg and the children are Catholic, I feel the need to confess. I tell Ann I've quit writing.

She's surprised and a little concerned. I've been a writer—or wanted to be one—as long as she's known me. "What will you do?"

I tell her about Echo Lake. "My second interview's Tuesday."

"Won't you be on the road?"

"Deep in the heart of Texas," I say.

She smiles, supportive. "Well, good luck."

It hasn't occurred to me I might need it.

Easter morning. Another extravagantly beautiful day. I slip into the boys' room with the robin-egg-blue bag of Easter candy I brought and set it next to Ross's pillow. I pat his shoulder and tell him he has to wake up. He groans.

"We want to make San Antonio before it gets dark," I remind him.

He grunts and rolls over. I head downstairs to get coffee. Greg has tucked a three-by-five card on the door to the fridge:

Claudia:

Loved having you & Ross here. He is a great young man. Wish all of you the best & hope to see you again soon.

Love, Greg

I'm struck by the phrase "young man." I've always thought of Ross as a boy, but yes, this weekend I glimpsed a young man. And Ross saw the child that I used to be.

I slip the card in my pocket and pour myself a cup of chicory coffee.

A few minutes later, Ross stumbles, half awake, into the kitchen, wearing the same shorts he came in, clean socks, and his dark green Frostbreaker Ultimate T-shirt from the one tournament that I've seen. He holds up the bag of Easter goodies I gave him.

"Thanks, Mom." He kisses my cheek.

"You're welcome," I say, touching the place that he kissed. "But eat something healthy. We have to leave soon."

He pours a bowl of corn flakes and milk and slumps at the table.

Ann appears, dressed for Mass—a black skirt and jacket with tiny white flecks.

Greg Jr. bounds down the stairs right behind her. "Mom! Do I look all right?"

Ann glances at his gray knit shirt and jeans, a quick diagnosis. "It's Easter. You'll have to look better than that."

"Aw, *man* . . ." He darts back upstairs.

I pull out our guidebook. "Know any good hotels in San Antonio?"

"I've stayed at a few on the river," she says, "but they're pretty pricey."

"Scrap that," I say. "This road trip's a bit of a financial white-knuckle ride."

Ann chuckles at my choice of language. "Been there."

"Hell," I say, flipping pages, "I've never been anywhere else." She and Ross stare at me.

I smile. "Speaking of puling thumb-sucking self-pity."

I notice that San Antonio's oldest motel, the Park Inn—built in 1935, when my mother was six—is only forty-five bucks a night. I read Ross the blurb, "'The rooms are nothing fancy, but they're clean and comfortable and some have delightful details such as the original Mexican-tiled floor.'"

Ross nods. "Floors are good."

I call and reserve a room for two nights, then we say goodbye to the kids. Scott's still sacked out on the floor by Ann's bed, so I kiss him softly on his downy cheek. He smiles serenely.

Ann walks us out to the car.

Ross, my somnambulist son, shuffles toward the passenger door, duffel and Easter candy in hand. "You drive," he says.

I laugh. "Good idea." I toss my overnight bag in the back, get in, and roll down the window.

Ann hunkers down by my side of the car. "This is so cool what you're doing with Ross."

"I hope so," I say. *You have no idea how much I hope so.* "And, hey, it was his idea. He wants to see our old trotting ground."

Her face clouds a little. "Kingsville's changed. It could mess up your memories."

"Don't mess with Texas?"

"I'd hate it to change the things you remember." She stands up. "Okay, you've been warned." She peers in my window. "Bye, Ross."

"Bye, Ann," he says, his eyelids at half-mast. "Thanks for everything. The zoo. Galatoire's."

"Any time." She slaps the window and steps back. "You two have fun."

"Come with us," I say.

"Oh, I *wish*."

"We'll do Kingsville, the sequel."

"I can't," she says, clearly torn. "I've got clinic and teaching." I thank her for taking the weekend off for us. "Mah pleasure," she says in her best Texas accent.

I back out of the live oak-lined driveway, blowing kisses to Ann, and drive away down the canopy road.

Ross closes his eyes. "I *love* those people."

"Me, too," I say, a little *verklempt*.

"But remind me *never* to be a doctor."

I glance over at him. "Too much hecticity?"

He smiles. "Right." He coined the expression when he was twelve, an accidental conflation of "electricity" and "hectic," but a perfect description of how it feels to be frantic.

I wind my way back to Interstate 10. Most of the traffic is eastbound to the city, the masses going to Mass, I assume.

I head west. "We're doing it, Ross. We're going to Texas!"

He doesn't answer. He's fast asleep.

Saturday, April 11, 1998

Trip budget: **$685.94**

Zoo/Roman candy: −$3.50 (cash)
Zoo/McDonald's: −$5.42 (cash)
Easter candy for Ross: −$8.76 (cash)

Balance remaining: **$668.26**

CHAPTER EIGHT

I-10, Louisiana

Ross sleeps.

He sleeps as we drive past the southern lip of Lake Ponchartrain.

He sleeps as we drive west over wetlands on long concrete bridges that cut through the tops of bald cypress trees. The Spanish moss looks like tangled hair that needs brushing. The mist is beginning to clear. I can see the bayou below, yellow butterweed dotting the pond scum that isn't pond scum at all—it's a carpet of duckweed, one of nature's smallest flowering plants.

He sleeps as we drive past the Bonnet Carré Wildlife Management Area, rich in raccoon, otter, bear, flying squirrel, but increasingly poor in red wolf and cougar.

He sleeps as we drive past Lake Maurepas, the resurrection fern bright green on the banks—a fitting sight on this Easter morning—and the water hyacinths so thick in places it looks like a carpet of lavender orchids.

Water hyacinth is Louisiana's own kudzu—an invasive species run amok—loosed upon Louisiana in 1884 at the International

Cotton Exposition of New Orleans, where visitors received one of the lavender flowers as a souvenir, a memento, and the hyacinth flourished in fountains and ponds and pools in the city and the countryside beyond to the bayous where a single plant doubled every two weeks, producing 65,000 other plants in one season, choking the water's natural flow, photosynthesis, food chain. A hundred and one years ago, this lovely lavender flower, flora's Helen of Troy, launched a thousand engineers (as in Army Corps of) who declared war on the plant, attacking first with pitchfork, later dynamite, flame throwers, and arsenic, the latter getting into the food of the workers, killing one man and leaving thirteen others critically ill. The hyacinth *thrived* in the poison and the pitchfork-cleared water and came back nine inches taller after the burn. And when dynamite destroyed everything else in the bayou, the hyacinth seeds germinated deep in the water. Two years later the plant rose again.

Talk about *resurrection*.

Ross sleeps as I-10 turns north-northwest at Sorrento, paralleling the Mississippi, if anything can parallel a river with zigzags half a mile wide.

He sleeps as I-10 heads west again, joins Interstate 12, and crosses the river at Baton Rouge. I brace myself as the Mystique starts up the high arching bridge, that *click click click* feeling again. *Don't look down, don't look down*, I think, gripping the wheel, but I came on this road trip in part to look, so I do. Below us, the water's slag gray. Industry sprawls to the south until the river cuts a sharp left and heads back to New Orleans. To the north I can see Louisiana's Capitol building, where Huey Long—"Every man a King"—was assassinated in 1935.

I crest the top of the bridge. "Ross," I whisper. "The Mississippi."

He mutters something and turns his face toward his window.

"Wake up," I insist. "It's the *Mississippi*."

"Mmm," he says, barely lifting his eyelids, then adds, mono-tone. "Oh, yeah. Wow. I saw it last month."

Of course. The Demented Ultimate Freaks came here for the 11th Annual Mardi Gras Baton Rouge Ultimate Tournament. The T-shirt's still on Ross's bedroom floor.

I feel a flash of resentment toward Ultimate, not so much for stealing my thunder here on the river but for stealing my *son*. If he hadn't fallen in love with the sport—and he's clearly in love—he might not be leaving home a year early.

Ah, I think, descending the bridge, *leave thy mother and cleave unto thy Frisbee.*

The bridge sets us down in Port Allen. I glance at Ross, sound asleep, the morning sun bringing out his hair's copper highlights, and I feel that frustration, that distance, again. Sleep feels like another barrier he's put up between us. But maybe it isn't. This semester he wrote a paper about the sleep needs of teens:

> Some researchers suggest that the normal circadian rhythm of adolescents is reset along with other changes of puberty, resulting in their rising later in the morning and going to bed later at night. . . . That is why teens sleep until noon, if not later.

Still, I can't help noticing what other mothers have told me—when teens are passengers with their parents, they have narcolepsy in cars.

Carcolepsy?

He sleeps while I drive halfway across Louisiana. Fast, slow, fast, slow. Construction. Heavy holiday traffic. It's taking forever to cross the state, broad at the bottom, the southeastern part sticking out like a Southern belle's bustle. And I have to pee and would kill for more coffee, so I pick up the pace, passing cars, trucks, RVs, and setting an awful example, but Ross is asleep so he'll never know. Finally, I give up, pull into a rest stop, park the Mystique in the shade, and turn off the engine.

Ross opens his eyes. "Driving kinda fast there, weren't you, Mom?"

I come out of the rest stop a few moments later. Ross is leaning against the driver's side door in his Frostbreaker T-shirt and rumpled seersucker shorts.

"What's wrong?" he says, catching my scowl.

"No coffee. So much holiday traffic, they ran out."

"Geez, Mom, you're an addict." He opens the back door and pulls out a Frisbee. "Here, I'll wake you up." He grabs my arm and pulls me across the parking lot toward a green grassy field.

"No, Ross, I need *coffee*."

"Come on. I'm gonna teach you something cool."

"We don't have time."

"Sure we do."

"We need to get to San Antonio while it's still light."

"We will."

"I don't want another Mr. Toad's Wild Ride like we had coming into New Orleans."

"Mom, relax. We're going to get there." He pulls me onto the damp grass and puts his hands on my shoulders. "Stay." He backs up with the Frisbee. "Catch."

"Woof," I say.

He tosses a nice easy backhand.

I catch the disc and toss him a backhand. "Okay, I'm awake."

"*Mom.*" He tosses a forehand, smooth and level. He makes it look easy. "You try it," he says.

"I can't."

He stops. Stares. "Excuse me?" All his life, when he and Anne would say, "I can't," I'd say, "Excuse me?" as if I didn't understand what they meant. Now my parenting's come back to haunt me. The chickens come home to roost.

"Okay, I'll try."

"That's the spirit! And you could be good, 'cause it's just like a forehand in tennis."

Tennis, I think wistfully—my sports bliss. I fell in love with tennis when I was eleven and Kingsville's summer rec program offered free lessons. I was the best in the program and played passionately from fifth grade through my senior year, when I won state runner-up in singles and doubles. And Ross was born with a golden arm, too, but he never loved it. He played for a while at Maclay, but he quit because his teammates "were a bunch of rich assholes. Snobs." And he doesn't suffer snobs gladly.

"Think footwork," he says. "Step into the toss."

I step. The Frisbee wobbles and falls.

"With the *right* foot." He lopes over to me and picks up the disc. "And you're not holding it right. Rest your index and middle finger up under the rim. Support it."

I do.

"Can you feel that?"

"I think so."

"Now step forward as you flick your wrist." He backs up.

I step forward and flick. The disc sails toward him . . . over his head. It lands in the parking lot, scraping the pavement, and disappears under a car.

Ross cracks up.

"What's so funny?" I say, a little crestfallen. I thought that showed real improvement.

"The first commandment of Ultimate!" He drops on all fours by the car like a Marine about to do push-ups, reaches under the car, and pulls out the disc. He stands, dusting off. Both of his Band-Aids hang loose at the knee. He rips them off, revealing pink but healed scrapes, and tosses the Band-Aids into a trash can.

"What's the first commandment?"

"'The most powerful force in the world is that of a disc straining to land directly under a car, just beyond reach.' This force is technically termed 'car suck.'"

"*Mom* sucks."

He slings his arm over my shoulder and gives me a squeeze. "No, hey, you were great."

"*Puh!*" I say.

"No, really."

I give him a long level look—*don't patronize me.*

"Okay, you were good. Let's try it again."

"Let's go to Texas."

"Just one more," he says. "It's the tenth commandment: 'The single most difficult move with a disc is to put it down.'" He sprints back to the grass.

I should walk to the car, insist that we go. If I don't, I know what will happen. He'll push until it isn't fun anymore. Like his hugs, on the rare occasion he hugs me—he squeezes so long and so hard I can hear my joints creak. Chiropractic hugs, I call them.

I have to beg for release. But I look at him now, bouncing on the damp grass on the balls of his feet—*love me, love my sport.*

"Okay." I walk back to the grass. "Just a couple."

He hands me the Frisbee and backs up again. I try holding it the way that he taught me, feel the pad of my middle finger in the crook of the disc where it curves down into the rim. I step into the toss, flick my wrist, and it sails straight to him.

He catches it, smiling. "See? That's a respectable forehand!" He backs up and throws a low forehand back.

I catch and throw it—wide right.

He dives and slides and catches the disc—a beautiful layout. He stands up grinning, his shorts streaked with grass stains. He tosses a hammer, and it *is* an overhead motion like serving in tennis. The disc hits the end of my finger—a quick *ʒing* of pain—and falls on the grass.

"Rub it, rub it," Ross shouts, the advice I gave him and Anne when they were little and hurt themselves.

I shake my hand and suck on my finger. I pick up the Frisbee and fling a long backhand. It sails high and hovers above him. Ross leaps and snatches it out of the air and throws it back before he hits the ground. The disc floats into my hands. I float back a forehand, the motion feeling more natural now.

He throws, I catch.

I throw, he catches, bobbing and weaving, more graceful than I've ever seen him—his pole vaults look like a public electrocution.

He throws, I catch, bobbing and weaving a little myself. The breeze feels cool on my face. The boughs of the dogwoods rise and fall like the wings of birds in an updraft.

Catch, throw. Throw, catch. We fall into a rhythm.

A dance.

CHAPTER NINE

I-10, Louisiana

Wide awake, Ross offers to drive.

"No drafting," I tell him.

His eyes narrow. "No backseat driving." Our eyes meet across the top of the Mystique. "Deal?"

"Deal." I toss him the car keys.

We get in, and he merges back on Interstate 10. We're east of Lafayette now. The traffic is bumper to bumper, but Ross keeps his distance. I close my eyes and drift back in time, remembering falling asleep in the car when my mother and father and sister and I left Pensacola to move to DC. I can remember resting my head on my father's shoulder when he carried me out to the car in the cool, dark early morning. He'd fashioned a plywood platform that fit across the floor of the backseat, and my mother made a pallet for me. Patty was already sleeping on the back seat. I remember lying on the pallet listening to the *whoosh* of the road right below me as we headed north, and the lovely sound of my parents talking in front. It's my only memory of my parents together. A year later they were divorced. Two years after that, Patty and I flew to Texas.

It occurs to me now as I open my eyes and look down on the Atchafalaya River's muddy brown water that we probably flew over these bayous on our way to Corpus Christi. If I'd stopped caressing the blond hair on Granddaddy's arm long enough to look out the window, I might have seen this watery land that, from the air, looks like a great splintered mirror. Seven years' bad luck. Eight, in our case. But not all the years in Texas were bad.

"Corpus was my hell, but Kingsville was my heaven," my mother said.

I tell Ross about arriving at Mamaw and Granddaddy's house, stepping up on the front porch, touching the cool wrought-iron grillwork while Granddaddy unlocked the door. "Inside the shades and curtains were drawn tight. They usually were. The house was so gloomy. Even the backyard felt closed in with its tall wooden privacy fence and Mamaw's flower beds of lantana, a smell that depresses me to this day."

Ross passes a bright yellow semi without a trailer. "How long did you stay at their house?"

"Two weeks. Until Mom arrived from DC. Mamaw seemed better. Granddaddy kept to himself. One morning I wandered into the kitchen and opened the door out to the garage. He was sitting there in his workshop, head bent, his auburn hair in the lamplight, building two beautiful desks, smaller versions of his own drafting table. I asked him who they were for, and he said, 'Two little foxes.' I remember standing there thinking, *Those lucky foxes!*"

Ross guffaws. "You fell for that? Two little foxes?"

"Hey, I was seven—one year older than Scott. I lived a very rich imaginative life."

"Like that's changed," he snickers.

"Christmas morning, when I saw those desks by our tree, I was just blown away."

Ross slows down for construction. Orange cones. One-lane traffic.

I offer him a malted-milk egg—speckled robin-egg blue—and eat one myself. "Mamaw enrolled us in the neighborhood school, Sam Houston Elementary, right up the road from their house. Patty started fifth grade. I started second and felt that displaced feeling again. I wanted to fit in so badly, and out on the playground, I saw a way."

"How?" Ross fishes out some more candy.

"Hula hoops."

He laughs. "Hula hoops?"

"Oh, baby, they were the *rage*. The few kids who owned one were king. Bingo! Instant popularity. Everyone else lined up at recess, begging for turns. And I remember standing there thinking, *If I had one, they'd line up for me*. The minute Mom got to Corpus I started working on her. Never mind that money was tight. Never mind that she was trying to find a rental house we could afford—and she did, on Austin Street, right around the corner from Aunt Patty and Jeff and Jon. I *had* to have a Hula Hoop of my own. The weekend we moved into our rent house, she finally caved."

"She bought you one?"

"Pink and white striped. I could barely sleep Sunday night. Monday morning, I took it to my new school, Fisher Elementary School, because we'd moved to a different school district. At recess I grabbed my Hula Hoop and raced out to the playground and waited for kids to line up and beg me for turns, but they walked past shooting me looks—*what's wrong with this chick?*

"Why?"

"At Fisher, Hula Hoops were *passé*. Over and out."

"Aww," Ross says sincerely.

"I felt like the biggest loser on earth. After school, I went home and hid the Hula Hoop in my closet. I felt so guilty about making Mom spend that money. I knew she didn't have it to spare. We didn't even own a car when we lived in Corpus."

"No *car*?" he says, amazed. Even now, living on a tight budget, we have more than one car.

"Sweetheart, we couldn't afford one."

Ross passes a van with an elaborate tiger face painted on the spare tire's cover. "What did you do?"

"Granddaddy loaned us his old Studebaker."

I hear my mother's voice, recounting that part of our story:

It was a little rusty Studebaker, but God, it was four wheels and an engine. Of course the brakes failed several times when I was driving. It was a wreck. It worried me because I didn't want y'all in the car. But it was all I had, and I didn't have any money.

"But any time Mom pissed him off, he'd take it away."

"That sucks."

"She thought so. It made her so mad she'd get tears in her eyes. Here she was, a grown woman, twenty-nine, with two children, and he was still yanking her chain. Even when he was sober, he could be a real bully. A fascist. He even looked a little like Hitler. Thin. Five-six, max."

"A mustache?" Ross says wryly.

"As a matter of fact. But blond and bushy—a cookie-duster,

they called it. And he was a real macho sportsman. Lived for hunting and fishing. When Mom got to Corpus, he insisted on taking us fishing out in the bay."

I tell Ross what my mother told me:

He'd get bees in his bonnet. Nothing would do but we had to go fishing. We must all be a family. But it wasn't a family, it was a nightmare. It was like a sentence of death going with him. But if I didn't, all hell would break loose, and then it was my fault. Mother said, "If you don't go, he'll start drinking. If you don't go with him, he'll make me go." Oh, I got my belly full of that. I told her, "If I have to go with him, you're going, too." But I told her this was the last time I'd go. I shouted, "As long as I live, don't you ever suggest I go with him again!"

Ross pulls back in the right lane.

"I remember Granddaddy driving us out Ocean Drive to the boat launch. I was in the back seat between Patty and Mom, who was sitting stock-still. So was Mamaw in the front seat. Both their backs rigid, neither saying a word because of that big fight about going fishing they'd had that morning. They barely spoke the rest of the day. Then Mamaw just sat on the boat staring back at the shore, scared to death because she couldn't swim. Mom didn't fish either. Patty and I did. I remember Granddaddy baiting our hooks with shrimp, but I don't remember catching a thing. And it was hot. So hot you could eat your own skin. South Texas, late August."

"Hotter than Florida?"

"Believe it or not. Granddaddy wore a straw hat with a green visor sewed in, but the rest of us were bareheaded. We all blistered, but Granddaddy refused to go in, even when my mother got sick."

"From the motion?"

"And the mistake she'd made coming back."

April 12, 1998, Easter Sunday

Trip budget:	**$668.26**
Gas:	−$9.33 (Visa)
Balance remaining:	**$658.93**

CHAPTER TEN

I-10, Louisiana

"Tabasco!" Ross shouts, pointing at a billboard for the factory on Avery Island. Tabasco is one of his passions. "Can we go?"

"I doubt it's open on Easter Sunday."

"On the way back?"

"Maybe," I say, sidestepping a promise. "If we have time."

We're approaching Lafayette now. Cajun country. The construction's much lighter. Ross is driving at a good clip—seventy-seven.

He tips his seat back a notch. "So what happened when you got back from fishing?"

I look over at him, his sunglasses hiding his eyes. "You really want to know?" I don't want to burden him with dark stories I didn't want to hear at his age.

"This is my heritage, Mom. These are stories I'll tell my children."

It's another one of those times when your child takes you by surprise, revealing depths you did not know existed. Ross has never mentioned children before (he won't even talk about *girls*), but it's clear that he sees himself as a father someday, as a link between the past and the future.

"Mom says you don't know who you are until you know where you came from—the places and people. Who they were, the choices they made, good and bad. If you know, you're free to make your own choices. If you don't know, you may not be making free choices at all."

Ross cocks his head, thoughtful.

I tell him about the day on Austin Street when Mamaw came over acting dead drunk and fell down our front steps and just sat there, disheveled. "Mom knew something was wrong because Mamaw was always so put together. You've seen the picture of her in my study." It's a photo straight out of *Gatsby*—Mamaw's exquisitely beautiful face, pursed lips and pencil-thin eyebrows, framed by a dark marcel wave, her slender neck draped in fur.

He pushes his sunglasses up on his head. "The one where she looks like a heroin addict?"

"Jesus, Ross!" I stare at him, shocked, not that he said it but that he *saw* it. In the photo, Mamaw's eyes—pale hazel, almost yellow—look anxious, trapped, haunted. "She was," I tell him.

His dark lashes rise. "A *heroin* addict?"

"Not heroin, no. Uppers and downers—Seconal, Miltown—prescribed by her doctor. But Mom didn't know until Mamaw fell down the steps, and Aunt Patty said it was probably drugs. Turned out, Mamaw was totally hooked. And who could blame her? That's how she coped with the violence. When Granddaddy cranked up the drinking, she cranked up the drugs."

"God," Ross says, "that's so sad."

"It was. A sad melodrama they played over and over while we lived in Corpus. *Long Day's Journey into Night*, Texas style."

"That play's so depressing."

"So was Corpus."

Ross drives in silence, a little too close to the back of a pickup truck tilting toward us under the weight of two yellow motorcycles in back.

"It's funny," I say.

He cuts me a look. "Is it?"

"Well, ironic. Mom didn't worry about the sixties teaching Patty and me to do drugs. She was worried we'd learn that from her parents."

Where do you think kids in the sixties learned to do drugs? From their parents! I remember crossing campus in the sixties and seeing stoned students and thinking, *Looks just like home!*

"How much did she tell you about all of that? When you were a kid?"

"She told us about Granddaddy's drinking—there was no hiding that—but she told us Mamaw was a hypochondriac. She kept Mamaw's addiction—and the violence—from us as long as she could. But kids know when something's wrong. Remember how you'd get stomachaches when you were little because I was upset?"

"Yeah," Ross says. He swings into the left lane and passes the pickup.

"Must be genetic, because I'd get stomachaches when we went over to Mamaw and Granddaddy's house. And I developed these weird nervous habits. All through second grade I had this high-pitched nervous whistle that sounded like spaceships landing in some Ed Wood movie."

Ross laughs.

"In third grade, I graduated to clicking my teeth. I'd sit in the back of the classroom and click my right molars together, then I'd have to click my left molars because you can't click the right ones without clicking the left ones—"

"For balance."

"Exactly. And one day the teacher saw me moving my mouth and thought I was talking and made me go stand out on the breeze-way."

"Poor *Mom*."

"The one time I *wasn't* talking and I got nailed for it."

Ross laughs again.

"Oh, yeah, I was pathetic. This little tightly wound fly-apart person. Sometimes I wonder if I would've been less of a wreck if Mom had leveled with us."

"You might've been worse."

We both laugh.

I gaze across the Gulf coast plain. "It's hard being a parent when you're taking care of your own."

"Like you're doing now," he says with compassion.

My eyes well, I'm so deeply touched. "Yes, or will be soon. It's so hard knowing the right thing to do. Mom thought she should shield us."

Ross returns to the right lane. "But who shielded her?"

"Mom and Aunt Patty played an elaborate shell game," I say as we pass Lafayette. "Their own little Underground Railroad. Out of the blue, Mom would tell us we were going to stay at Aunt Patty's."

When the shit hit the fan Aunt Patty would take y'all over there, and I would deal with Mamaw and Granddaddy. Every time I turned around, Mamaw was on my front porch demanding I protect her from him. I'd have to get y'all over to Patty's, then I had to spend all night on the telephone. Granddaddy would call me on the phone every thirty minutes—"I'm coming out to blow your goddamn head off."

Ross winces. "How long would you stay?"

"As long as she needed to take care of Mamaw. Sometimes one night, sometimes two or three. I had a great time. My cousin Jeff was my age, and Jon was two years younger. My sister would stick her nose in a book—too old for our nonsense—but the boys and I would roller-skate up and down the cracked sidewalk. Or play Civil War."

Ross smiles. "Civil War?"

"Jeff and Jon had these really cool muskets that shot caps. We'd chase each other up and down the alley, blasting each other with caps and performing spectacular death scenes. When Mom's around the corner with Mamaw, worried sick that Granddaddy might shoot them."

"But you didn't know that."

"No. And most of the time, Jeff and I played Benny Benny."

"Benny Benny." Ross shakes his head, smiling. I've told him about the great sagas Jeff and I acted out with Jeff's stuffed blue rabbit, Benny, and my stuffed kangaroo, Kanga.

"Why Benny got top billing, I'll never know."

"Better agent," Ross says.

I laugh.

"And didn't you write a bunch of stories about a beatnik cat?"

"In fourth grade. We had to write a story each week, so I wrote a whole series."

"Like Clive Cussler."

"Only different."

He chuckles.

"Every time we'd study a new place—the Amazon, Egypt—that's where Gotee went in the next story."

"Gotee," Ross snickers.

"Hey, the class loved it. I remember the day I read one of my stories in front of the class, and they were laughing like crazy, and I thought, *This is it. This is what I want to do.*"

"Write," Ross says.

The word hangs between us.

"And speaking of Clive Cussler . . ." I slide in the next tape of *Shock Wave* and hit Play.

"I carried you away from the party before you had a chance to eat," Dirk Pitt says to Maeve. "Let me whip you up something."

"Lord," I say, "the man can cook, too?"

"He's Dirk Pitt, Mom."

"This is making me hungry."

Eyes on the road and one hand on the wheel, Ross fishes around in his robin-egg-blue Easter bag and pulls out his hand, palming a piece of candy. He unfolds his fingers, revealing a Cadbury egg.

"Thanks, baby." I pluck it from the palm of his hand and carefully peel back the red, green, and blue foil. I bite the end off the egg and taste the sweet yellow center.

Maeve declines Dirk Pitt's offer to cook but accepts the Remy Martin he pours for her before he sits beside her on the couch. "She wanted him desperately, wanted to press herself into his arms, to just touch him—"

"Okeydokey," I interject, turning it off before Dirk Pitt's turned on. "My turn to drive. And I bet we can find some great Cajun music."

"Yeah," Ross says, pulling over. The tilted truck with the yellow motorcycles rumbles by as we switch places.

Back in the passenger seat, Ross scans the radio stations: Easter services, oldies.

"Enough of this corporate radio shit." He switches from FM to AM and—*voila!*—a local Cajun radio station is going full blast with "Bosco Stomp," one of my all-time favorites.

I pull back onto the highway. The DJ chats for a while in Franglais with a woman named Betty. I catch a few words like *bonjour* and *dimanche*. Then he plays "Jolie Blonde." I start singing along in my terrible French. Ross joins in, and we rock out until we go out of range just east of Lake Charles.

It's the last town of any size before Texas. High noon. We're both starving, never mind the candy we've eaten. Ross pulls out our guidebook and looks for a restaurant.

"How about Paw Paw's?"

"*Dites-moi.*"

Ross reads aloud from the guidebook. "'Paw Paw's. 300 US 171. 11 a.m. to 11 p.m. Reservations accepted. Cajun menu.'"

"I'm there."

He continues to read. "'Semi-à-la-carte: lunch $7.95 to $12.95.'" He glances at me, aware of our shoestring budget.

"Hey, it's our last chance to eat Cajun."

He reads on: "'Three dining rooms with nautical theme; shrimp boat in pond. Family owned. No cr crds accepted.'"

That's how Ross reads it: cr crds.

I reach over and ruffle his hair. "You crazy child."

We find Paw Paw's, a sagging blue building with a rusty beached shrimp boat listing to starboard. The pond has dried up.

Ross frowns. "Not a good sign."

"Hang on." I get out and read the hand-painted sign on the door and report back to Ross. "The restaurant's closed because Paw Paw's passed on."

Ross pulls a long, tragic face. "Paw Paw's *dead?*"

I nod, solemn. "Gone to that great Paw Paw patch in the sky."

Nothing else seems to be open on Easter Sunday, so we swallow our pride and pull into Taco Bell, twice a travesty because we're in Louisiana and the food isn't Cajun, and we're spitting distance to Texas and it ain't real Tex-Mex. Not the enchiladas, frijoles, and tacos Ann and I used to eat with our mothers at El Jardin. But it's here and it's cheap and we're *hongry*.

"Hey, more money for Texas," Ross says, closing the guidebook. "And nothing could have topped Galatoire's."

Full of gorditos, we make a run for the Texas border. I serenade Ross with the songs I learned as a kid—"Deep in the Heart of Texas," "I'm Going to Leave Old Texas Now," "Texas Our Texas"—stopping mid-song to explain that the lyrics had to be changed from "largest and grandest" to "boldest and grandest" when I was in elementary school because Alaska had just become a state. "Really pissed Texans off." Then I sing my all-time favorite, "The Ballad of the Alamo." I learned every tearjerker verse by heart as a girl when John Wayne's *Alamo* came to the Texas Theater in Kingsville.

Ross raises an eyebrow at the song's cornball lyrics. "I think Clive Cussler wrote *that*."

I laugh and finish singing the song, crooning a truly bad imitation of Marty Robbins's mellifluous voice for the taps-melody finish.

Ross stares, a little amazed at his mother.

"You didn't know I wanted to be a torch singer?"

The truth is, we're both a little moved by the story of the Alamo told in this sappy song.

And sap rising, Ross masks emotion in true family form. "Did you see the Far Side cartoon?"

"Which one?"

"Christmas 1836. Santa Anna's son gets the original coonskin cap."

I swat his right arm—*swat, swat, swat, swat!*—as we pass a gigantic sign:

TEXAS WELCOMES YOU

And just like that, we're in Texas.

April 12, 1998, Easter Sunday

Trip budget:	**$658.93**
Taco Bell:	−$7.97 (cash)
Balance remaining:	**$650.96**

PART TWO

CHAPTER ELEVEN

I-10, Texas

Across the sump of east Texas we go past Orange and Beaumont and on into Houston, shooting through the heart of the city. No wimpy bypass for us.

"Look!" Ross says, pointing south. "The Houston Astrodome!"

I smile. Last spring I took Anne to Florence. We sat in the Boboli Gardens overlooking the red-tile-roofed city dominated by Brunelleschi's splendid octagonal dome built to glorify *Santa Maria del Fiore*. But here in the South, for all the carrying on about Jesus, the domes that dominate city skylines are built to glorify sports.

We pass an exit to University Place, and I think of the six weeks my mother and sister and I lived here when I was thirteen, but that's a piece of the story I'll tell Ross later. Still, it's the first family landmark in Texas I've seen and I feel the same sensation I felt when we passed Pensacola: I'm driving straight toward my childhood.

Out the west side of Houston, past Katy, Brookshire, Sealy, Columbus, across the dry windy hills. Weimer, Flatonia. The traffic is lighter. We're tracing the line that separates north from south Texas—that part of the state from the San Antonio River to the Rio

Grande, the part that looks like an upside-down dorsal fin. I see patches of yellow lanceleaf coreopsis and pink evening primrose, big as poppies. Blue sage, blackfoot daisy, but not a bluebonnet in sight.

"Rats," I tell Ross. "I wanted to show you bluebonnets."

"Maybe it's too late in the season?"

"I hope not."

A gas station looms into sight. I glance at the gas gauge—less than a quarter of a tank. "I think we'd better gas up."

"I'll pump, you pay," Ross says.

I pull in. We get out. The wind is blowing so hard it whistles. I remember the south Texas wind. Like the Wallace Stegner quotation I keep on my desk:

Across its empty miles pours the pushing and shouldering wind, a thing you tighten into as a trout tightens into fast water.

Ross fills the tank while I go inside and find a detailed map of San Antonio. I find a whole rack—Rand McNally—and pick one of those flat fold-up maps I know once opened will never be folded correctly again. I pay for the map and the gas, step outside, and tighten into the wind.

We head west, the sun sliding down the big Texas sky. Soon San Antonio appears in the distance. "There it is, boyo. The city where our Texas story began. Where Mamaw's and Granddaddy's families—the Cattanachs and the Morgans—settled like so much flotsam and jetsam on the banks of the San Antonio River."

Ross frowns. "Why do you say flotsam and jetsam?"

"I didn't mean to sound derogatory. Just that both families were broke. They came to San Antonio in the wake of financial ruin."

Driving the last stretch to the city, I tell him what my mother told me about Mamaw's parents—Big Mama and Dada—immigrating from Scotland in 1903 with their eight children, though baby Benjamin died on the way. "Poor Big Mama," I say.

"Poor baby Benjamin," Ross adds sadly.

"Yes. May he—may they all—be reborn in happier times."

I tell him how poor they were, how the children often went hungry, because Big Dada gave half his income to the religious zealot he followed from Stornoway in the Outer Hebrides. How the children woke up Christmas mornings and found no presents under the tree.

For some reason, this detail gets me. I burst into tears.

"Oh, Mom," Ross says with sincere sympathy. "Are you okay?"

I swipe away tears. "There are so many unhappy children in our family story." *Including you*, I want to say, but I don't. I rifle my purse and pull out a Kleenex.

Ross pats my arm. "But you weren't unhappy, were you, Mom?"

"No. Once we got to Kingsville. Thanks to my mother. She broke the cycle of abuse and neglect."

We're driving into San Antonio now, the city where my mother was born. City lights blink on across the lavender sky. "Help me find the exit for Broadway."

But Ross points at a big white loaf of a building dominating the skyline. "The Alamodome!"

"That's one weird looking dome," I say. "It looks like some creature lying flat on its back, its legs sticking up in the air."

Ross sits up straight in his seat. "You think the Spurs are playing tomorrow?" He's more excited than I've seen him this trip.

"Dunno," I say. "If you want, we'll find out." *If he wants*. A blind woman could see that this boy is *dying* to see the Spurs play.

I wouldn't mind seeing a Spurs game myself. I was a David Robinson fan when he played for Navy.

"If they're playing, can we go?"

"We'll see," I say, again avoiding a promise I might not be able to keep. But I feel that *zing* of adventure. I have no idea if we'll be at a Spurs game tomorrow. Or where we'll be eating tonight. How this trip will turn out. How the interview with Echo Lake will go day after tomorrow. How Kingsville will look after thirty-two years.

The San Antonio skyline slides by on our right. The Tower of the Americas—leftover from the 1968 Hemisfair—casts an eerie green glow.

Ross looks back as we sail past the exit to Broadway. "That was our turn."

I slap the steering wheel, "Damn damn damn *damn!*" The sun's down. The last light is going.

"It's okay, Mom, lighten up."

"Yeah, you're right." I don't want to get lost in the dark but I don't want to lose my cool, either, or Ross's overriding memory of this trip might be his mother's meltdowns.

I take the next exit, the off-ramp looping through a field of long golden grass. We're way the hell west of town, almost out in the country, but it doesn't take long to backtrack to Broadway where, as our guidebook promised, we find the Park Inn with its five-hundred-year-old live oak out front.

April 12, 1998, Easter Sunday

Trip budget:	**$650.96**
Gas and map:	−$11.38
Balance remaining:	**$639.58**

CHAPTER TWELVE

The Park Inn

Ross looks at the yellowed tourist brochures for the San Antonio Zoo and Six Flags Over Texas while I pay for two nights.

"Do you know if the Spurs are playing tomorrow?" he asks the elderly woman checking us in.

"No, honey, I don't," she says sweetly. "I don't keep up with all that."

The antique telephone switchboard behind her lights up.

"Excuse me a minute." She connects the caller to the party they've asked for.

I feel like a girl back in Kingsville watching Lily Tomlin on *Laugh In*: "Is this the party to whom I am speaking?"

She slides the Visa slip across the counter. "If you want to place a call, just pick up the phone in your room and I'll connect you."

"Thank you," I say, signing the slip.

She hands me a tarnished brass key.

Before the Bates Motel there was the Park Inn, I think when I unlock our door and it creaks open. The room looks and smells like a cave—dank, dark, decayed. I can feel the undertow of depression like I used to feel at Mamaw and Granddaddy's house.

I click on a lamp. The plastic lampshade is crooked and yellow with age, almost orange. Chunks of the plastic are missing. The original Mexican-tile floor our guidebook promised is filthy. *Original to Santa Anna*, I think.

Ross walks in with our bags and starts to drop them on the floor, but I stop him. "How 'bout you put those up on our beds?"

At Lily Tomlin's recommendation, we eat up the street at Earl Abel's, one of the oldest restaurants in town. It's getting late, almost closing time. We order the fried chicken dinner, something we could get anywhere in the South, but we're tired and hungry and not thinking clearly.

While we wait for our food, I tell Ross about Granddaddy's family coming to Texas. "His father, Doctor Franklin Morgan, bought a ranch in Port Lavaca, a crazy move for a self-taught engineer from Chicago."

"You just said he was a doctor," Ross says, confused.

"He was *named* Doctor."

Ross laughs. "No pressure there."

"Mom said he was brilliant—a pioneer in designing new ways to heat homes. Invented boiler valves, that kind of thing, and made more than one fortune, but he lost most of it because he didn't patent his inventions either."

"That's probably where Granddaddy got it."

"And where he learned to be mean. Doctor Franklin—DF for short—was mean as a snake. Threatened to kill Granddaddy all the time when he was a boy."

Ross flinches. "The sins of the father."

"And the mother. Granny wasn't much better."

I tell Ross what Mom told me about Granddaddy's child-hood:

He was raised with no sense of self-worth. Oh, worse than no self-esteem. Absolutely brutalized from the time he was a small child. If he did anything wrong, they'd beat the shit out of him. He'd get behind the bathtub—one of those old tubs up on claws—and try to get away, but Granny would corner him and beat him with a quirt—a braided leather dog or pony whip. It's no wonder Dad was so disturbed. Such a delinquent. While he was growing up on the ranch, prob-ably around puberty, they bought him brand new cowboy boots—exquisite leather. He sat in elementary class and cut them to pieces with a pocketknife. DF beat the shit out of him with a bullwhip. They bought Dad a new rifle. He didn't know what to shoot, so he went over to the next pasture and shot a $500 prize Brahma bull, right between the eyes. Dad didn't think it would hurt it because it was only a .22, but the bull dropped dead right there.

"He *killed* it?"

"Dead as a doornail. The rancher came over and asked DF if he knew who killed his prize bull. Granddaddy didn't dare say, or his father would've killed him for sure."

The waiter sets down our food. We're the last customers of the night, so it's no wonder that the chicken is overcooked and the mashed potatoes are dried out and lumpy.

"Eventually DF lost the ranch and moved his family here."

"To San Antonio."

"Right. And he and Granny made Granddaddy drop out of school in eighth grade and support them."

"They *made* him drop out?"

I can see in Ross's green eyes that he's processing this. "Yes, and Mamaw's parents made her drop out, too—in seventh grade. She had to go to work and give them the money."

"That's *child labor*."

I nod. "And this was before the Depression."

Ross lets out a whistle.

Our waiter refills our water and joins the other waiters who sag against the bordello-red wall, their body language betraying their thoughts: *Come on, lady, take your kid and go home.*

I remember it's Easter Sunday, no doubt one of their busiest days of the year. No wonder they're exhausted. We are, too, after ten hours of driving, so we skip dessert, pay our bill, and walk back to the Park Inn.

I unlock the door to our dismal room, let us in, and lock it again.

Ross does what he always does in motels—heads for the TV. "There's no remote!" A cry of despair.

"Sure there is." Then I look at the television, which looks like the one we had back in Kingsville when I was a girl. "Sweetie, they hadn't *invented* remotes when that TV was made."

Ross turns it on the old-fashioned way. The picture slowly appears on the dusty screen.

I try to close the vertical blinds, but the plastic wand is long gone and some of the vertical strips are missing. I try to close the gaps by tugging and pulling, but they won't close completely. Any slob who saunters down Broadway can look in our window.

"Maybe we'd better turn off the lights," I tell Ross. "God knows, the room will look better that way." I reach under the broken plastic shade and click off the lamp. Bars of light from the PARK INN sign out front slant through the gap-toothed vertical blinds.

Cathode rays start to strobe across Ross's face.

"The picture's *flipping*," he says, about to flip out.

"Try the vertical button."

"The what?"

I turn the lamp back on and show him the button. He fiddles with it but the picture keeps flipping. He smacks the TV with the flat of his hand. The picture flips faster.

"Easy, fella," I say. I shove my suitcase to the edge of my bed and prop up my pillow—the approximate size and softness of a fifty-pound bag of cement.

Ross gives up and falls back on the bed, hits his head on his pillow and cries out in pain. He hefts the pillow up and down. "I've never seen anything this hard classified as a pillow. They should register it as a *weapon*." He flings it back on the bed and flops on his stomach, staring gloomily at the flipping screen. *Flip flip flip flip.* He gets up and turns the TV off. "This place *sucks*."

I turn off the lamp.

"I wish we could go back to Ann's house."

The leviathan feelings of failure lurking under the surface since we left Tallahassee threaten to breach. Oh, I have never wanted or worked for material gain. I have never thought that it matters, and I have never compared my life to Ann's. But now, sitting in this dingy motel, I see the two of us up in her mesquite tree when we were ten, confiding our dreams of what we wanted to be, and I can't help comparing how they turned out—Ann's mansion the measure of her success, and this shabby shit hole the measure of mine.

Thar she blows!

"Look," I tell Ross, "I'm sorry as hell we have to stay in this sinkhole, but I'm not the success that Ann is."

"Yes, you *are*, Mom."

"*Puh!* I failed as a writer."

"No, Mom, you *quit*."

A car pulls up out front, its headlights raking our room. Ross's face is pinched with exhaustion and anger. The car lights snap off. Our room's dark again. But I can feel Ross withdrawing. The fragile closeness I've started to feel is slipping away, the distance between us returning.

I feel panic rising. *I can't let this happen. Not on this road trip.* I grope under the lampshade and turn on the light.

Ross blinks. "What are you doing?"

"We're changing hotels." I grab our guidebook.

"It's almost eleven."

I flip pages. "Then we'll get a different place for tomorrow."

"You paid for two nights."

"Then I'll get a refund!"

My eye falls on the listing for the Menger Hotel: "'Its location, smack between the Alamo and the Rivercenter Mall and a block from the River Walk, is perfect. Its history is fascinating.'"

"You want to see the Alamo, right?"

"Right."

"Good! We'll stay at the Menger. We can park the car and walk everywhere." Then I notice the price: $122–$142 a night. We'll be broke before the week's over. Financial flotsam and jetsam, just like everyone else in the family—Big Mama and Dada, Granny and DF, Mamaw and Granddaddy, and my mother when I was a child. Here I am with my own child four decades later and not a damned thing has changed—*back in Texas pinching pennies again!* But we're *not* staying here after tonight. Maybe the Menger has some kind of discount for state employees.

I reach for the phone, and I gape. If you dusted for prints, Alexander Graham Bell's would turn up. There's no dial. Then I remember what Lily Tomlin told me: "If you want to place a call, pick up, I'll connect you." But I can't ask her to give me the Menger.

I grab my purse, check for change. "Come on," I tell Ross.

He stares blankly at me.

"Off your ass and on your feet!" One of my father's favorite military expressions.

In one motion Ross stands and shoves his feet in his untied running shoes. "Where are we going?"

"To find a pay phone."

"And a newspaper!" he says. Laces dragging, he follows me out the door.

This stretch of Broadway looks seedier now that it's dark. We cross the street, dodging cars, and walk to a convenience store down the block. Seedier still. We go in.

The surly clerk sits surrounded by gum, cigarettes, chewing tobacco, and soon-to-be day-old candy.

I look around. "Do you have a pay phone?"

"It's outside," he grumbles.

On our way out, by the door, Ross sees a stack of the Sunday *San Antonio Express-News*. He flips to the sports page. "Mom!" he shouts, exultant. "The Spurs *are* playing tomorrow! They're playing the *Lakers*!"

"Yeah, but David Robinson won't be playing," the clerk says

lugubriously. "Sombitch Karl Malone took him out in Salt Lake City."

Ross's spirits aren't dampened. He follows me out the door, his face ecstatic. "Could you call about tickets?"

"Okay," I say. "First the Menger, then the Spurs."

I see the two blue pay phones between the gas pumps and Broadway. One is in use—a man shouting obscenities at his girlfriend or wife or ex-wife. I think of Granddaddy but shake it off and step up to the other phone. I slide in a quarter and dime and punch in the number I wrote down for the Menger. Beside me, the man hawks and spits. I close my eyes, cross my fingers, and ask the receptionist if they have a discount for state employees.

"Sure do," he says, nice and friendly.

"How much is a double room?"

"Seventy dollars a night."

I cover the phone and whisper to Ross, "It's only nineteen more bucks than the Park Inn!"

He gives me a triumphant thumbs-up.

I cross my fingers again and ask if they have a room for tomorrow.

"How about 402?"

"Does it have two double beds?"

"They're king size," he says proudly, the subtext clear: This *is* Texas we're talking about.

"Book it," I say and give him my cr crd number.

Ross bounces on the balls of his feet.

"And could you give me the number for the Spurs ticket office?" He does, but when I drop in another quarter and dime and punch in that number, I get a recording. I hang up.

"What?" Ross asks, disappointed.

"They're closed for the day."

"Will you call in the morning?" Ross asks as we walk back up Broadway.

"Yes."

"First thing?"

"First thing." A promise, but I don't know when I've seen the boy so excited.

Back at the Park Inn, I let him into our room and head to the office and break the bad news to Lily. "I'm afraid we'll only be staying one night."

She looks deeply hurt. "You don't like it here?"

"Oh, no, that's not it at all," I say, a bald-face lie. "My mother was raised in San Antonio, and I just talked to her, and she said we *must* spend a night at the Menger." A half-truth—my mother *was* raised in San Antonio.

"Ah," Lily says, pouting.

I hand her my cr crd for the cr.

Back in the room, I lock our door and try to use the slide bolt, but it's only held on by one flimsy screw. I give up and turn out the lights and get ready for bed. When I slide under the covers, my head barely makes a dent in the pillow.

Ross bounds out of the bathroom and hops in bed. "'Night, Mom," he says.

"Goodnight, boyo."

"And you'll call the Spurs."

"First thing in the morning."

"And get tickets."

"I promise." It slips out before I can stop it.

"Momzilla," he says happily. In a moment, his breathing becomes even and deep.

I say a small prayer that the Spurs aren't sold out.

April 12, 1998, Easter Sunday

Trip budget: **$639.58**

Park Motel: -$103.50 (Visa)
Earl Abel's: -$ 17.70 (Visa)
Phone/snacks: -$ 7.97 (cash)
Park Motel (credit):   +$ 51.75

Balance remaining: **$562.16**

CHAPTER THIRTEEN

San Antonio, North Broadway

"Is it time to call yet?"

"Soon," I say. "The Spurs ticket office opens at nine."

Ross glances up at the clock—quarter till—and pours on more blueberry syrup.

We're sitting in a booth at the IHOP, north Broadway, eating breakfast—pancakes, eggs, bacon, orange juice for Ross, and coffee for me. Fresh from the shower at the Park Inn, he's put on a clean T-shirt—green and black tie-dye—the same sea-foam green as his eyes. His damp hair is dark brown. Umber? Burnt sienna?

"God, Mom," he says, setting down the glass pitcher of syrup. "Do you know how cool it will be to go to a Spurs-Lakers game? The week before the playoffs? To be able to tell my friends at Maclay I was *there*." A fierce pride crosses his face, and I sense something deeper, some hurt or rejection, but I know it's best not to ask. "It will *make* this trip for me."

And that's what I want more than anything else—to buy two

Spurs-Lakers tickets and make this trip for him. But what if I can't make it happen? I pick at a dried drip of blueberry syrup on the side of my plate. "I can't guarantee there will be tickets left."

"Mom," Ross says, "you promised." His eyes are bright with belief that I will conjure two tickets. Momzilla. As if a mother-son promise has magical powers. He looks at the clock again—ten of nine.

Our waiter warms up my coffee. "God bless you," I say and ask for the check. It's almost nine when he brings it. We pay up front. The lanky young manager thanks us.

Ross and I walk to the pay phone in the IHOP foyer. Outside it's gray, a light drizzle. "Cross your fingers," I say, fishing for change. Wishing I owned a cell phone. It was bad enough when calls cost a quarter, but now you have to find a dime, too. I'm surprised Texans didn't contest the rate hike. Once, when change machines that only gave ninety-five cents back for a buck appeared in Texas airports, enraged Texans ripped the machines off the wall.

Don't mess with Texas!

I can only find a quarter. I look at Ross. "Brother can you spare a dime?" All he has are nickels and pennies. I pull out a small stack of credit cards in my purse. Dimes, like memories, can be tucked away where you least expect them. Sure enough, I find one thin dime stuck between my driver's license and Visa card. A torch on one side of the coin, FDR on the other; 1981, the year Ross was born.

I slide in the quarter, wait for the *clink* when it drops, then carefully drop in the dime. *Plink*. I've lost a small fortune at vending machines and pay phones. I could swear that the coin slots turn up in a smile when they see me coming.

I hear a dial tone and punch in the number. The recording I heard last night tells me they open at nine.

"It's five *past*," Ross says.

"And I've lost thirty-five cents." I give him a dollar. The manager gives him some change. I try two more times—another seventy cents—until the Spurs box is finally open.

The woman there tells me I can't purchase tickets from them over the phone. "You have to call Ticketmaster." She gives me the number.

Clink plink. Ticketmaster is busy. I try again and again, carefully feeding the money and pressing each number—no redial on payphones—but the line is still busy.

Ross watches, anxious. He wants these tickets badly, but our one full sightseeing day in San Antonio is slipping away.

I deposit the quarter and dime and punch in the number, now burned in my brain. Busy. I press Coin Return. The quarter drops. The dime doesn't. I push it again. Nothing. "Damn it!" I slap the pay phone with the side of my hand.

"Easy, fella," Ross says.

The dime *plinks* into the coin return slot. I slide it out and start over. Busy, busy, and busy again. "Oh, come *on*," I moan, understanding why Texans rip things off the wall.

Ross senses a meltdown. "I'll wait in the car."

I keep trying—quarter, dime, dial tone, number—only to hear the busy signal again and again—*beep beep beep beep*. I rest my forehead on the cool metal casing and ask the universe if it's really so much skin off its nose if I buy two Spurs-Lakers tickets and make this boy's trip? Apparently so. When I try again, the line is still busy. I try to stay cool. I count the small blessings—at least I'm not standing out in the rain at a pay phone. No one is swearing or hawking and spitting. Or waiting here to use this pay phone.

I keep trying. Five minutes. Ten.

The manager peers in at me, amazed I'm still trying.

I look out the window at Ross, sprawled across the passenger seat of the Mystique, the door open, listening to corporate radio shit. It's way past nine now. I could stand here at this pay phone the whole precious day and still not get through. I press Coin Return one more time and fish out the quarter and dime and slide them in the slot nice and slow to give whoever's hogging the line a little more time to hang up.

The phone rings! A young man says, "Ticketmaster."

Overjoyed, I ask if he has any Spurs-Lakers tickets. "Some," he says.

I sag with relief. "I need two."

"What section?"

"*El cheapo.*"

"Sorry, the cheap seats are gone. Well, I've got a couple but they're not together. Are you willing to sit apart?"

"No." I can't imagine seeing this game without Ross beside me. I want seats together. Great seats, if that's all we can get. "What else have you got?"

"Courtside," he says.

Oh, I can see it—Ross and me sitting courtside! I feel reckless—*to hell with the budget*! "How much?"

"Three hundred apiece."

Times two is more than we have left in our budget. "Anything in between?"

"Hang on, I'll check." He's not the sharpest knife in the drawer, as Ross likes to say, but he's kind and helpful and patient. It takes ten more precious minutes, but he finally comes up with two seats in the corner for thirty-four dollars each.

"Lock and load!"

"Let's see, that'll be thirty-four times two, plus our fee. Totals out at, with tax . . . seventy-nine eighty."

I give him my cr crd number, and we close the deal. I hang up, exhausted but also elated. I walk to the IHOP's front door and swing it wide open. "Ross! We got them! Fourteen rows up from the court!"

"Momzilla!" he crows, rolling out of the car and rushing up to me with a hand-stinging high five and a bone-crushing hug.

The manager comes into the foyer and congratulates us. Ross high fives him, too.

"How's parking at the Alamodome?" I ask him.

"A nightmare," he says. He pulls out his wallet and hands me the card of a taxi driver he knows. "Give Al a call. He'll take you there and pick you up when the game's over."

"Like the monkey peeing in the cash register," as my dad loved to say. "This is gonna run into money."

But Ross looks so damn happy, I don't even care.

Next stop, the San Antonio Zoo. Monkey Island. But there's only one lone baboon eating grass on a flat rock, and one mountain goat covetously eyeballing the grass. The baboon leaps up and runs at the goat waving its hairy arms, the long reddish-brown hair swinging like the fringe on a western jacket. The goat retreats. The baboon settles back down to eating.

"Shoot," I say. "When I came here as a girl, there were *dozens* of monkeys."

"And how would they sound, Mom?" he says, smiling at me. He knows my repertoire of animal sounds, and Monkey Island is one of my favorites—a convincing mix of maniacal laughter and chitter-chatter.

I cut loose with it now, but the baboon does not miss a chew.

The mountain goat gazes at me then back at the grass the baboon is eating. Ross chuckles, shaking his head, telegraphing what he told me and Ann in New Orleans: *You could entertain yourself forever in a world all your own.*

We wander through Amazonia and the reptile house, stopping to watch a pit viper retracting its fangs—in, out, in, out.

I laugh. "It looks like Jerome Staggers."

"He was bucktoothed?" Ross deadpans.

We admire the endangered white rhinos in the African Plains, but the warthog and lion and tiger cages are empty because zoo employees are hosing them down.

"Talk about vanishing species," Ross says glumly.

After the Audubon Zoo in New Orleans, this feels like a ghost town—that forlorn morning-after-the-big-party look. And for good reason, I realize, when I see the *San Antonio Express-News* for sale in front of the gift shop. There was a big Easter celebration here in the park yesterday.

A headline catches my eye: TRAGEDY IN BRACKENRIDGE PARK. I scan the article below:

> Tragedy struck a family celebrating Easter Sunday in Brackenridge Park when a 9-year-old girl drowned in the San Antonio River after slipping through the fingers of the man who had just saved her friend. "I had the little girl in my hand, but I couldn't hold her because I lost air," said Ernesto Vargas, who had been picnicking with his family in the park. "I lost her."

I turn and see Ross making faces at the golden lion tamarin monkeys, their reddish-blond manes fanning out around their silver-dollar-size faces.

I ambush him with a kiss on the cheek. "Whattayasay we get outta this place?"

He flashes a tiny, tolerant smile.

Leaving Brackenridge Park, I turn north on Broadway.

"The Menger's south, Mom."

"I have to photograph my mother's house in Alamo Heights."

"We only have one day in this city!"

"Ross," I say, "I promised."

312 Alta Avenue. I pull up in front of the handsome frame house, freshly painted dark gray with light gray trim. A deep front porch with four light-gray pillars. A limestone chimney. A one-car garage. The yard's nicely landscaped—red geraniums in the bed around the oak tree out front. But I can't shake the feeling it's haunted, this house where my mother used to run to the window when her father got home.

"I was maybe in fourth grade," she told me.

I'd run to the window to look at his face when he got home and see if he was in a drunken rage. That frightening face. The jaw muscle flexing. I remember feeling terribly relieved if it wasn't.

The house where Granddaddy's drinking went out of control.

I remember one day Daddy was in the back room, drunk as a lord. Mother told me she was going to take him up to this place in Houston that would cure him. She told me to go to my room and shut the door because she didn't want me to see him. But I opened the door and looked, and his feet were dragging down the hall as she carried him. I was ten or eleven, just sick at my stomach. I was smart enough to know how bad it was. I remember the feeling of the pits watching my father being dragged down the hall. I remember her face, the strain of trying to carry his drunken body. She had to put him in the car, and she was terrified the neighbors would see. You know, you look at these people. You depend on them. And Mother having to hold him like that. She took him all the way to Houston, got him into the hospital. This was a Friday. Sunday morning the doorbell rang, and I opened the door and said, "Daddy, what are you doing here?" Mother was standing in the kitchen. She couldn't deal with it. She went to pieces.

The house my mother begged her mother to leave.

He'd slap her around and threaten her and scream at her. Really, how much can you take of that? It went on all our lives, but his drinking and rage became deadly on Alta. I begged and pleaded with her to leave. She said we couldn't afford it. She didn't feel she could support us. I said I'd do anything, wait tables, if we could just have a home that was peaceful. She wouldn't do it. She said, "No, no, we're not that kind of people." But look at what we were. She'd live in a fantasy world when reality was beating her in the face.

The house where Granddaddy stalked his own family.

Stalker? That was one of his favorite games. I remember him screaming, "I'm gonna kill all of you tonight!" He used to stalk us through the house with a .30-30 deer rifle. Or the shotgun he took hunting. Or several .22s, one a single-shot rifle, one with a scope and repeater. And I'll never forget waking up early one morning. He and Mother had been going at it hammer and tong, and he was standing by my bed with a .22 rifle. I remember lying there looking at him. He was looking at me with such hatred. I didn't know what he planned to do. I didn't know if he had killed Mother. I knew if I showed fear, he'd kill me, but my only fear was that he'd killed Mother. So I tried to ignore him. I rolled over and pretended that I was asleep. This is why I have flashbacks still to this day. I'll be doing something and all of a sudden I get this picture—I'm twelve years old, and we're living on Alta Avenue, and he's trying to kill her. It's always connected to my fear he would kill her.

But I don't tell Ross any of this. I can tell by the set of his jaw he's not in the mood. I'll take the photo and go. "Have you seen the camera?"

He scowls. "Checked your butt?"

I let this go and find the camera on the floor of the backseat. "Would you be in the picture?"

Ross shoots me that look—*not just no but hell no.*

"Come on. It's for Mimaw."

He slides out of the car and stands by the geranium bed and glowers at me, his arms open wide: *Okay, here I am. Are you happy?*

I snap the picture. "One more," I say, but he's already heading back to the car.

He gets in and slams the door, hard. "Remember the Alamo, Mom."

Monday, April 13, 1998

Trip budget:	**$562.16**
IHOP:	–$13.10 (Visa)
Ticketmaster:	–$79.80 (Visa)
Pay phone:	–$1.40 (cash)
Zoo:	–$18.98 (cash)
Balance remaining:	**$448.88**

CHAPTER FOURTEEN

San Antonio,
South Broadway

I'm struck with the strangest sensation when we walk in the Menger—I feel right at home. I can't explain it because I've never been in this hotel before, but I sense a connection. Being here feels meant to be. Charmed. And I can see that Ross feels it, too. He opens his arms wide and spins around slowly in the sprawling lobby.

"Mom," he says, laughing. "I *love* this place!"

The ruggedly handsome receptionist at Registration welcomes us like old friends, my favorite definition of a Texan being "someone who assumes a familiarity where there is none." I show him my FSU faculty card for the state-employee discount. It's not even noon, but he tells us we can have our room early. "It's all yours," he says, handing over two key cards and a snazzy gold brochure about the hotel.

I ask what's the best route to drive to the Alamodome.

He shoots me a boy-you-are-new-to-these-parts friendly smile. "You don't have to drive. It's three blocks away."

Ross and I look at each other—*charmed!*

Before we go to our room, we walk the length of the lobby. "Tasteful opulence," the tastefully opulent brochure calls it. The lobby overlooks the tropical gardens where Oscar Wilde strolled "wearing a lace-frilled black velvet coat, knee-length trousers, scarlet stockings, and silver-buckled slippers, sipping spiked lemonade and smoking long, foreign cigarettes."

We stroll past pillars and planters, across Oriental rugs on the highly polished dark wooden floor, and admire the carved beamed ceiling and the fireplace flanked by glass cases of historic "jackcorns and geegaws," as my mother says. The grand piano and the antique card tables and chairs are mahogany—a rich reddish-brown—the color, I realize, of Ross's hair.

Our spirits continue to rise as we ascend to our room in the elevator—first, second, third floor.

Ross reads from our guidebook as we walk down the hall, filling me in on the Alamodome. "'The locker rooms are 5,000 square feet. The roof covers *nine acres*.'"

I smile. "That good old Texas obsession with size."

"They give tours," he says. "Can we do that when we pick up our tickets?"

"You bet," I tell him, unlocking our door.

We step into our room, which seems like nine acres. We have our own dressing room and a Texas-sized bedroom with two king-size beds.

I open the drapes and the sliding-glass doors and step out on the balcony overlooking the pool. It's a sunny day, breezy. A Texas flag flaps on a flagpole.

Ross drops his duffel bag on the clean, carpeted floor at the foot of his bed, spreads his arms, and falls backwards onto the rose-covered spread. He flaps his arms as if he's making snow angels. "Seventy dollars!" he says, laughing at our good fortune.

I laugh, too, especially when I check out the tastefully opulent bathroom. It's only slightly smaller than our *room* at the Park Inn, with marble counters, brass fixtures, and baskets of fancy soaps and shampoos.

I walk back into the bedroom, so lovely, light, airy. The drapes billow. Ross is watching TV, a trailer for *As Good as It Gets*, Greg Kinnear asking Jack Nicholson, "Do you know where you're lucky?"

Ross sighs happily, "It doesn't get much better than this."

In the buckskin light of the Alamo's shrine, our euphoric mood settles. Ross stands in the stillness, head bowed, as he reads the account of the battle:

> The final assault came before daybreak on the morning of March 6, 1836, as columns of Mexican soldiers emerged from the predawn darkness and headed for the Alamo's walls . . . The desperate struggle continued until the defenders were overwhelmed. By sunrise the battle had ended and Santa Anna entered the Alamo compound to survey the scene of his victory.

I suspect the Far Side cartoon is far from Ross's mind now. He likes to say that he has no heroes, but I can see that he's deeply moved by the sacrifice of the men who died here. I'm moved, too—by the story and my son's response to it.

We cross the courtyard to the Long Barrack Museum, the site

of the last stand here at the Alamo. Inside, Ross moves slowly, absorbed by the details of the battle. I'm more absorbed by the offbeat details—how seventeenth-century Franciscan fathers dug irrigation ditches called *acequias* and turned this desert into a garden. El Jardin. "Alamo," I discover, means "cottonwood." In the early 1800s, the Spanish military named it in honor of their hometown, *Alamo de Parras*.

I feel that sense of connection again. San Antonio is my mother's hometown. She was born here, at P&S Hospital—Physicians and Surgeons—in 1929, the year of the Great Crash. Her childhood spanned the Depression. I remember what she said about Granddaddy finding work every day, and Mamaw finding ways to stretch the money he didn't drink up. I don't really have any heroes, either, but it hits me now that Mamaw's efforts—and Granddaddy's, too—were heroic.

Ross and I step outside, squinting into the bright sunlight. I see Joske's—now Dillards—on the other side of the Menger, and for a moment I can see Mamaw—a tall, slender beauty with that dark marcel wave—hurrying across Alamo Plaza to Joske's because the buyer she once worked for in the women's department had just called to say the new samples were in. Miss Harper loved Mamaw, my mother told me, and always gave her first choice—and the sample clothes for ninety-nine cents apiece—so that Mamaw, poor as she was, could look lovely.

"Mom? Hello? Lunch?"

I surface and look up at Ross.

"I'm *starving*," he says.

"Me, too," I realize. "Let's eat on the river."

"You wanted to find the Anaqua Grill," he reminds me.

I read about the restaurant in *Southern Living* before we left

Tallahassee. It sounded terrific, but it's in the Marriott a few blocks away.

"Nah," I say, "too much trouble." We walk toward the river. "So how did the Alamo strike you?"

"It's a cool story," Ross says. "To know there's a purpose. You know, something to die for." We walk down concrete stairs shaded by lush bougainvillea—yellow, orange, and fuchsia. "But it *sucked* that they wouldn't send reinforcements. I mean, they left their own men to die."

"Maybe the men were crazy to stay."

"I'd've stayed."

I stop as a wave of profoundly mixed feelings breaks over me—grief and pride—an archetypal ambivalence I suspect every mother across time has felt when her child insisted on going to war. "Would you?"

"Yes."

"Why?"

"Because of the cause."

"Texas independence?" My tone betrays that I would never trade my son for that, Texan though I may be.

Ross looks at me, surprised I don't get it. "No, Mom," he says. "*Freedom.*"

Monday, April 13, 1998

Trip budget: **$448.88**

The Menger Hotel: −$80.00 (Visa)
Alamo donation: −$1.00 (Visa)
Postcards: −$1.51 (cash)

Balance remaining: **$366.37**

CHAPTER FIFTEEN

Boudro's

"You know, Ross, there's all kinds of courage," I say, sipping fresh-squeezed limeade from a long-stem wineglass. "It's not just about battles and drawing lines in the sand."

We're sitting beside the river at Boudro's, famous for its *enchiladas verdes*, highly recommended by *The New Yorker*, the menu tells us, though I can't help smiling at that—since when were New Yorkers experts on Tex-Mex?

"I know, Mom," Ross says, clearly trying to head off a lecture. He slides his Oakleys up on his hair, more golden now under Boudro's umbrella, which is the approximate color and shape of a taco shell.

The waiter sets down two plates of green enchiladas. I take a bite. Okay, *The New Yorker* was right—they're delicious.

Ross splashes Tabasco on his.

Easy, I start to say, but I know he loves it hot. "Or maybe it is about lines in the sand. We all have our limit. I saw my mother hit hers in Corpus Christi."

"When?"

"1960. The fall of my fourth-grade year. The height of the Kennedy-Nixon campaign."

He sets down the Tabasco. "What was that like?"

"Suspenseful."

He laughs.

"Incredibly tense. All the kids at school were for Nixon, but Mom and Patty and I were passionate Kennedy fans. I paraded around wearing this fifty-cent-piece-sized Kennedy/Johnson campaign button. You've seen it in my study—the one with their faces on the front?"

Ross nods and takes a slug of his limeade. "Let's hang on to that button."

"Let's do," I agree, touched that he'd want to. "I thought I would die of suspense before the election. I'd put my nine-year-old ass on the line, and the race was too close to call." I put a dash of Tabasco on my enchiladas. "Ever hear of a TV show called *Dobie Gillis?*"

"Sure. With that beatnik."

"Maynard G. Krebs."

"Who went on to star in *Gilligan's Island.*"

I lean back and smile. "You are something, you know that?"

He smiles back.

"How do you know about *Dobie Gillis?*"

"Reruns."

"Did you see the episode where Maynard can see into the future?"

"Missed that one."

"They hyped it for weeks before the election because he was going to tell us the winner. I *lived* for that show. And when it aired, Maynard's about to make his big revelation when he has a crisis of conscience and decides it would be wrong if he told."

"Rip off!" Ross says.

"Bait and switch. I felt so burned when the episode ended. *Sucker!*"

"It's pretty funny you fell for it."

"Hey, I was nine. So I had to wait like the rest of the country and wear my big-ass button to school where I took no end of grief from my right-winger classmates. But that was nothing compared to the grief Mom took from her right-winger father."

I tell him about the Sunday dinner when my mother announced that she wasn't voting for Nixon. "Granddaddy went apeshit. Then Mamaw said she was voting for Kennedy, too. Granddaddy said she sure as hell *wasn't*. And that must've hit what was left of Mamaw's stubborn Scot streak, because she told him she would vote as she pleased—the Constitution guaranteed that—and she wanted to cancel out his vote for Nixon."

Ross hoots. "Good for her!"

"It was one of her finest moments. Of course, Granddaddy figured Mom was behind it, so he repo'd our car."

"Oh, man . . ."

"It was hard enough having to walk all the way to HEB to buy groceries and carry them home, but it made her crazy to think that she was thirty-one years old and he still controlled her. Or tried to."

"What did he say when Kennedy won?"

"Very little."

We laugh. Tourists glide by in tour boats, gazing at us.

"Mom realized she had to build a life for herself, and education would be her ticket out. Her independence. She'd been taking a few classes at Del Mar Junior College in Corpus and she'd fallen in love with history. She'd study at the kitchen table for hours. At dinner, she'd regale Patty and me about Richard II, the Princes in the Tower of London, you name it, until our eyes would glaze over, but she didn't notice until we pulled out imaginary paper and pretended to take notes."

Ross laughs. "You're going to hell, Mom."

"Oh, yeah. But nothing could dampen Mom's spirits. I've never seen *anyone* so passionate about learning. She was radiant. I wish you could've seen her—so young and pretty. Tall and thin. Freckled. Short dark hair, the same mahogany color as yours. And she dreamed of being a teacher. She said that had been her dream since she was a girl, right here in this town, when she lived on Alta."

"Amazing," Ross says.

"It is, isn't it?"

He nods. "And here we are now."

"It all comes full circle."

The silence that follows feel hallowed, both of us struck by the sacredness of our own family story. Around us, the lunch crowd at Boudro's is laughing and talking. Monkey Island.

I savor the last bite of my green enchilada and set down my fork. "So, after the election, Mom decided to step it up as a student, start taking more classes, and try to finish her education. But that cost more money. She took a part-time job before Christmas in the dish-and-stemware department of some store in Corpus— four-hour shifts while Patty and I were in school—and she started saving to pay for tuition. I remember Patty and I saved money for that Christmas, too."

"How much?"

"Seven dollars."

Ross laughs.

"It was a fortune for us, but we wanted to buy Mom a wonderful present."

"What was it?"

"An electric frying pan."

Ross cracks up.

"I remember how excited we were buying it and wrapping it up. We'd never given Mom a big present, and we wanted so badly for her to be happy."

"I know that feeling," Ross says.

"Do you?"

"That's why I wanted to go to the Anaqua Grill."

I look at him frowning at me, knitting those wooly-worm eyebrows that are just like my father's, and I feel a sweet stab of love for this boy. "Boudro's is fine. I *am* happy. Delicious food. Dappled light. Great company."

"I still wanted to go, Mom. For you." That fierce look again.

"I'm sorry, sweetheart," I say. "I didn't realize . . ."

The waiter busses our plates and brings us our check.

I finish the story. "Anyway, Christmas Eve finally came with Mom's present wrapped up under the tree, and Patty and I are back in our bedrooms trying to sleep when—*bang!*—we hear this pounding on the front door. We haul ass to see if it's Santa. Mom tells us to stay in the hall. Because Granddaddy's on the front porch screaming obscenities at her: 'If you're gonna read all those goddam books, you can damn well read these!' He pounds harder because he wants to give her a big box of Zane Grey novels."

"Zane Grey?"

"Genre stuff. If Clive Cussler wrote Westerns. But Mom didn't know what he had in the box so she's not about to let him come in, not after all the threats he's made, all the late-night phone calls saying he's coming over to blow our goddamn heads off."

"God, Mom."

"He's outside yelling, and Patty and I are hanging back in the hall in our jammies hearing all this. Patty's worried what the neighbors would think, and I'm worried we won't live to open our presents. And finally we hear Mom shout, 'Get off my porch, or I'll call the police!' And then there's silence."

"What happened?"

"He must've believed her because he left the box on the porch and went home."

Ross exhales. "Merry Christmas."

"It was, in spite of him, but I understand why my mother hates holidays."

Ross leans back. "How'd she like the frying pan?"

"Loved it."

Monday, April 13, 1998

Trip budget:	**$366.37**
Boudro's:	−$20.78 (Visa)
Balance remaining:	**$345.59**

CHAPTER SIXTEEN

The Alamodome

We have a few hours to kill before the Spurs box office opens, so we mosey along the riverwalk back to the Menger. On the way, we hit the Hard Rock Café to buy Ross a T-shirt, then we climb the stairs to the street, the temperature rising with each limestone step. The Alamo looms into view.

Ross lights up. "Let's go to the Alamo IMAX!"

I have to admit I'm a sucker for IMAX, and it seems so fitting for Texas—big, big, big, BIG!

We duck in the Menger's revolving brass-and-glass door, across the tastefully opulent lobby, down the long hallway, and out the back door to the IMAX theater where a showing of *Alamo . . . The Price of Freedom* is ready to start but we stop. The tickets are seven bucks each. My jaw tightens. Our tab is rising faster than the afternoon heat.

"Never mind," Ross says, trying not to sound disappointed. "We'll just cruise the mall."

But I remember something my mother said before we left

Tallahassee: "You can recover the money, but you can't recover the time." My jaw relaxes. "Let's do it," I say.

The script's cheesier than the acting, but the screen is four stories high, and the film sweeps us up in the battle and brings it to life. Ross is transfixed. I look at his face in the flickering light and remember being transported, too, when I was a kid and saw *The Alamo* at the Texas Theater the year we moved to Kingsville. John Wayne put his own money into the production, which pretty well tanked, even though the story's a Hollywood dream—nary a woman in sight and buckets of blood, everything except a happy ending. That came later, at San Jacinto.

Moved by the movie, we return to the Menger and change for the Spurs-Lakers game. Ross throws on his new Hard Rock T-shirt over his jeans. I opt for khaki slacks and a long-sleeved western-cut chambray shirt, in case the Alamodome has the air-conditioning blasting.

At five-thirty, we walk to the Alamodome and pick up our tickets at the box office. Ross asks about tours of the locker rooms, but the frail gray-haired woman says they're done for the day. Ross handles this well.

I hand him the tickets. "Take good care of these, boyo."

Reverently, he reads aloud what they say—Home Game 44/ San Antonio Spurs vs. Los Angeles Lakers—then tucks them deep in his jeans' front pocket.

We cross the broad plaza past a big fountain and look back at the Alamodome.

"Pretty impressive," Ross says.

"No kidding." The white Sta-Puft roof looks like more than nine acres, and the building has multiple levels. The middle level is glass. Tuxedoed waiters glide past the windows like tropical fish. Decked-out diners eat at tables draped in white linen. How I wish I could buy Ross an elegant dinner! "Let's eat there," I say wistfully.

"Oh, right," he sighs. "That'd cost more than the tickets." He looks at his watch and brightens. "Hey, let's go find the Anaqua Grill!"

"Sweetie, we don't have time—"

"Oh, come on, Mom! Tip-off's not for two hours." His face is sweet fierceness again.

"I'd love to," I say.

Ross has a way of walking when he's happy and proud—shoulders back, chest out, chin up. He walks that way now, the Spurs tickets safely tucked in his pocket, as we enter the Marriott lobby, a posh place with a casual lounge in the middle.

I see the Anaqua Grill on the opposite side overlooking a manicured garden full of peacocks and other exotic birds dressed a whole lot better than we are. The restaurant is elegant, understated, with jewel-tone votive candles on linen tablecloths that match the terra-cotta tile floor.

"Ross," I whisper, "we're underdressed."

"It doesn't matter," he says. "You deserve to eat here. You've come a long way."

He's right about that—halfway across the USA.

It's six o'clock. The Anaqua Grill is just opening for dinner. The maître d'—a stub of a man in an Italian silk suit—moves a music stand holding an elegant leather-bound menu aside so it's no longer blocking the entrance.

He glances at us, his first customers of the night, and I swear his lip curls. He walks away without saying a word. I look at the menu and my heart goes *squish squish*. *Southern Living* said meals here were six to eight dollars, but the subject was lunch. The average dinner entrée is thirty, except for the Chef's Pasta, which is only thirteen.

"We could split that," Ross says, reading my mind.

"Um, maybe," I say. I'm watching the maître d' in the back of the restaurant, whispering to a waiter, the two of them looking our way. *Lose the losers*, I imagine him hissing, then he moves silently through the shadows, lighting the candles, the sheen of his silk suit catching the light.

The waiter approaches in a tasteful tropical shirt. He's about Ross's height, thirty years old, max, but already balding, and his aquiline nose above the shirt's splashy colors makes me think of a parrot. "Good evening," he says, sniffing the air. I suspect he means it to be condescending, but it comes off a bit Boris Karloff.

"Good evening," I say. "We'd like to have dinner."

The waiter studies our running shoes—Ross's laces untied—his jeans, my khakis, his Hard Rock T-shirt, my chambray shirt. "Perhaps you'd prefer to eat in the lounge," he intones, gesturing toward the heart of the lobby where a half-dozen people dressed more like us slouch in overstuffed chairs and chow down on pizza. "I can recommend an *excellent* black bottom burger." He hands me a menu photocopied on bright turquoise paper.

I feel Ross bristle beside me. After five years in prep school, he doesn't suffer snobs gladly. He plants his feet and pulls himself up to full height—five feet eleven—like a rattlesnake coiled to strike. "*No*," he says, barely moving his lips, "we want to eat here in the Anaqua Grill. And we want to split the Chef's Pasta."

I've never seen him like this.

The waiter glances over his shoulder for reinforcements, but the maître d' is nowhere in sight. "Um, yes, sir," he says. "Come this way." He grabs two leather-bound menus and leads us to a table overlooking the garden. Peacocks wander, pecking the ground.

Ross offers me the chair facing out. He knows I love a good view.

I sit as gracefully as I can in my khaki slacks. "We just have an hour," I tell the waiter. "We have to make a Spurs game."

"Lovely," he says. Basketball fans. He looks like he just smelled a fart. "And what would you like to drink?"

"Water," we say together.

"Of course," he says curtly. And goes.

Outside the sun is dipping close to the arbor. A breeze lifts a grapevine. I look across the table at Ross, backlit by the sun, his face in six o'clock shadow, and I don't see a boy anymore. I see the man he's going to be. Or just became. Since my children were born, I've wished for them humor, kindness, and courage. Now I know that Ross has all three.

He looks at me. "What?"

"You. Standing up for me like that."

He lifts his nose, sniffs the air, a perfect mimic. "Perhaps you would prefer to eat in the lounge."

I laugh, shielding my eyes because the low sun is blinding, and I have a paranoid flash that the waiter picked this table on purpose. If it were just a foot to the left, the mullion would block the sun, and I wouldn't go blind. "Ross," I say sotto voce, "when the maître d' and the waiter aren't looking, we're moving the table a foot to the left."

"*Mom*," he says. He was ready to deck the son-of-a-bitch, but moving our table a foot to the left embarrasses him.

"Just do it." I see the maître d' turn his back. The waiter is nowhere in sight. "Now!" We lift the table and set it back down. I feel a cool stripe of shade on my face. "Ah," I say, "much better."

The waiter returns with our water. He looks at the table, the mullion, the table. I feign innocence. "It's such a beautiful restaurant," I say serenely.

"Thank you," the waiter says stiffly.

"Didn't I tell you?" I say to Ross, then, to the waiter, "I read about it in *Southern Living*."

The waiter looks startled. "*Southern Living?*"

"Did you see the piece?"

"Um, no," he stammers.

"You should see it. A nice little write-up."

"I'll have to get that issue," he says, stumbling slightly as he rushes off to the kitchen.

Ross and I exchange glances, baffled.

The waiter races back with a plate of speckled sliced bread. "This is our pesto bread with sun-dried tomatoes," he says, bowing slightly. "I think you'll like it."

I lean into the aroma of warm bread and basil.

"And I think you'll be pleased with the Chef's Pasta tonight," he says with newfound respect.

"Um, lovely," I say, trying to figure out why he's done this one-eighty. Nothing about us has changed since he thought we were no one, and now he's convinced that we're someone.

The waiter hurries back to the kitchen.

"Ross," I whisper. "When I said, 'I read about it in *Southern Living*,' I think he heard, 'I *wrote* about it.'"

Ross laughs, nice and wicked. "Well, you are a writer."

Was, I start to say, but I let it go, enjoying this rich irony—I quit writing because I felt like a failure, but now, because the waiter *thinks* I'm a writer, he's fawning like I'm some big success. And I'm pleased as a parent because Ross has witnessed, in record time, both sides of snobbery—the supercilious and the servile.

A second waiter in a tropical shirt appears in the garden and starts feeding the peacocks—a show, I suspect, just for us.

"He's a bit crazy," our waiter confides, confidential, when he returns to refill our water. "But the birds love him."

"Ah," I say, smiling at Ross—*He's schmoozing us now.*

A few minutes later, with great ceremony, our waiter sets down two large white pasta bowls filled with sun-dried tomato fettuc-cini—a beautiful palette for the pale-yellow saffron cream sauce, the gray oysters, the gray-green New Zealand mussels, the bright-green grilled asparagus, the two bold brushstrokes of chives shoot-ing over the end of each bowl, and the bright red crawdad on top of the pasta.

Ross shoots me a look, and I know what he's thinking—*This ain't the thirteen-buck special.*

"This is half?" I ask the waiter politely.

"Well, the chef was a bit *generous*," he says. "Because you're sharing." He bows. *Bows.* "Enjoy."

We do. The saffron is subtle, the mussels and oysters are fresh and delicious, the asparagus is permeated with the smell of mes-quite smoke, and the crawdad is a sweet, salty cross between lobster and crab.

Ross's eyelashes flutter as he puts a morsel of New Zealand mussel into his mouth. "I'm in heaven," he murmurs, "and we still have a Spurs game to go to."

We savor our food until seven, hardly saying a word, and I know what William Blake means by "eternity in an hour." Outside in the garden, a peacock spreads its iridescent blue and green tail and pirouettes a slow circle like some supermodel. The sun sinks behind the arbor, leaving us in soft, pale saffron light. An exotic peahen—white with gold feathers—struts past the window like an enchanted creature in an emperor's garden.

"I didn't know birds came in those colors," Ross says. The loud primary colors of his Hard Rock T-shirt have softened in the late-evening light. *All Is One*, it says in a semicircle over the logo.

There's so much food, we can't finish. I glance at my watch. Tip-off is twenty minutes away. I signal to the waiter, who brings a small leather-bound folder and sets it softly on the table beside me.

"When you're ready," he says in a hushed voice.

Ross eyeballs the folder.

"Whatever it costs, it's worth it," I assure him. I open the leather folder and peek at the bottom line. I let my jaw drop and push it back into place.

Ross blanches. "How much."

I smile. "Fourteen dollars."

He laughs. "*Fourteen dollars?*"

"And one cent," I say.

The waiter thanks us profusely and personally escorts us across the lobby to the door closest to the Alamodome. "The best way is to go east on Durango."

But the traffic is heavy, loud, dusty. We decide to cut through the Hemisfair grounds. Pink and yellow hibiscus bob in the balmy spring air. We weird ourselves out by standing at the bottom of the Tower of the Americas and looking straight up until it seems to be falling.

"It's so *high*," Ross says.

So are we—on this trip, this day, the crazy way it's worked out. Like this shortcut. We walk over a rise and lo, there's the Alamodome.

We merge with hordes of fans streaming into the game.

"Who are we rooting for?" I ask Ross.

"*Mom.* When in *Rome.* You always root for the home team."

"Okay, okay, I'll root for the Spurs. When I work for Echo Lake in LA, I'll root for the Lakers."

A bald man tears our tickets, and I part with five bucks for a program, a slick NBA publication with a photo of the Bulls and the Lakers on the cover.

"This is a *Spurs* game," Ross says, indignant.

Worse, the feature interview is with Karl Malone—spawn of Satan in this town since he KO'd David Robinson. But the fans aren't just pissed off at Malone. They're pissed off at the Spurs for not getting back at the Jazz when Malone messed with Texas and took Robinson out. The national media has branded the Spurs a "soft team."

"What the Spurs are lacking . . . an ENFORCER!" one fan said in our Sunday paper. And San Antonio columnist Kevin O'Keefe, who swore he abhorred violence in sports, said, "The essence of being a team is to take care of a teammate who has been wronged. . . . What DIDN'T happen Wednesday night in Salt Lake City is why the reputation exists . . . and why it will continue to do so."

I follow Ross into the arena, an explosion of music and bright colors—hot pink, chartreuse, international orange—that strikes me as more Miami than Texas. A wall of electric-blue curtains divides the home court from the rest of the Alamodome. A huge scoreboard with monitors facing all four directions hangs above center court.

Ross shucks and jives to the music (he was voted Best Dancer at Maclay) as we descend to our seats. "Mom, these are *awesome*." They're tucked in the corner—a familiar TV angle—almost eye-level with the basketball goal.

"We could've been there." I point to the high-dollar seats I thought about buying—folding chairs lined up along the side of the court to our right, where the Spurs cheerleaders, the Silver Dancers, are bumping and grinding.

"No," Ross says as we settle into our seats. "I like these better."

I smile. "Good answer."

The Spurs trot onto the court in home white. We stand and cheer with the rest of the crowd. The Lakers follow, wearing deep blue with a gold running stripe. Scattered boos. We toss in a few of our own. David Robinson isn't dressed out. At tip-off, he paces in front of the Spurs' bench in the biggest beige suit I've ever seen.

The Spurs get the tip, and the players thunder our way.

"These guys are *sequoias*," I whisper to Ross.

Shaquille O'Neal looks like a giant bald genie. He's David Robinson's height—seven one—but looks twice as wide at 320 lbs. Still, he's damn graceful—on fire, in fact—scoring twenty-three points in the first half. The Spurs play the Lakers close for a while—rookie Tim Duncan matching Shaquille in points and rebounds—but with nine seconds left in the first quarter, Van Exel hits a three-pointer, igniting a nine-point Laker run that Kobe Bryant caps with a dunk. The Lakers lead at halftime, 37–28.

"That's lower scoring than *college*," Ross moans. It's his first NBA game, and I know he wants something bigger, big as the players, the Alamodome, but I have this terrible feeling it ain't gonna happen without Robinson.

For our halftime entertainment, a couple of dancing quick-change artists spin and whirl center court, then the monitors broadcast a spoof on Jerry Springer featuring a shrieking marital fight between the Spurs' mascot, Coyote—crazed green eyes, open mouth, red tongue lolling—and his coyote wife. On screen, she hurls herself at him and starts beating him up. The picture blinks out and—*bang!*—a bandaged Coyote on crutches hobbles onto the court right below us, Mrs. Coyote hot on his trail. She grabs one of his crutches and whacks him.

The crowd roars with laughter. Children wave stuffed Coyotes around in the air. I notice Ross noticing them.

"Would you like one?"

"I'll just go see what they cost." He races off but returns empty-handed. "They're *twenty dollars*."

"So what?" I say, and I mean it. "We just saved that on dinner. C'mon, it can be your Spurs souvenir."

"Nah," he says, sitting down. The second half is about to begin.

The Spurs start to chip away at the Lakers' lead, closing the gap to five points with a 7–0 surge punctuated by a Jaren Jackson three-pointer.

The arena rocks as hope rises, but the Spurs hit a cold streak, shooting a lousy 30 percent. The Lakers shoot 50-plus. The scoring gap widens. The Lakers' lead hits double digits. The home crowd's mood starts to sour.

So does the Spurs'. With 4:46 left in the game, Kobe Bryant slam dunks, and Laker guard Derek Fisher runs through the lane smack into Will Perdue. The crowd howls for a foul. No call. Perdue grabs Fisher and swings him around and throws him down on the ground. Fisher leaps up and pushes Perdue, and they both start throwing wild punches.

Ross is on his feet shouting, "Yeah! That's more like it!"

So is the rest of the crowd. They're going crazy, egging Will Perdue on, but the officials break the two players apart and eject them both from the game. The crowd cheers for Perdue as he leaves the court.

Play resumes—for forty seconds—then Monty Williams grabs Van Exel's head with both hands and flings him onto the floor. Van Exel leaps to his feet and grabs Williams' head and hurls *him* down. Shaquille barges into the brawl, and the rest of the Spurs and Lakers swarm off the bench.

"WrestleMania!" Ross shouts, his face glowing, ecstatic. It's beyond his wildest dreams—when his friends at Maclay speak of this brawl, Ross can say he was *there*.

The Spurs fans are howling for blood. Ross and I are howling with laughter. I have this guilt flash that I should set a better example, at least *pretend* to be upset by the violence, but it looks like something you see on cartoons—a blur of bodies and fists and exclamation points flying. I've never seen overgrown men act like this. A giant snowball of supersized players starts to roll toward the stands—*crash!*—toppling fans and folding chairs in the high-dollar seats. The Silver Dancers scatter like minnows.

"Glad I didn't buy courtside seats," I shout into Ross's ear.

"*Really,*" he replies, laughing.

Williams and Van Exel are ejected. Van Exel shakes his middle finger at a Spurs fan. The crowd boos. The refs let Shaquille play. The crowd cries for more blood, but O'Neal answers with back-to-back slams, and that's all she wrote. The Spurs are shellacked—or Shaquilled. Lakers 99, Spurs 75.

But as Ross and I walk back toward downtown with the rest of the Spurs fans, along the broad walkway that passes under I-37, I notice a strange serenity in the crowd, a serenity usually reserved for the winners.

Ross explains, "The Spurs lost the game, but they won the *fight.*"

Back at the Menger, we feel serene, too. I call room service and order two servings of their house specialty—mango ice cream. Hang the cost! Our guidebook says that President Clinton liked it so much he had it flown into DC for his inauguration.

Ross and I sprawl on our sprawling beds in our sprawling room, savoring the pale orange ice cream piled high in glass goblets.

"It's better than Dole Whips at Disney World," Ross says, the highest compliment he can confer. He sets the empty goblet aside, flops on his stomach, and flips on the TV.

"*Look out!*" shouts the announcer on *Sports Center* as images of the brawl we just saw flash on the screen.

Ross roars with laughter again as the gigantic ball of supersized bodies rolls toward the stands and fans and cheerleaders scatter. He looks happier than he's been this whole road trip.

Watching him, I feel the same way. He may forget everything else about this trip with his mother when he leaves home in a year, but I know he'll remember this day in my mother's hometown.

I reach for the phone, take a chance that it isn't too late, and punch in Mom's number. She answers, relieved that we're safe. "Guess where I am," I ask her.

"Texas," she says.

"San Antonio. At the Menger."

"The Menger!" She laughs. "My father air-conditioned the Menger."

I blink. "Granddaddy?"

"Back in the thirties. He used to take me there with him when I was a girl. I'd play in the lobby while he worked on the job, then he'd buy a Coke for me and a beer for himself, and we'd sit in the garden. Or at the bar."

My mind is, in a word, *blown*.

"Have you and Ross seen the Menger Bar?"

"No."

"It's a beauty—an exact replica of London's House of Lords pub—but historic in its own right. Teddy Roosevelt recruited his Rough Riders there. More cattle deals were made in that bar than anywhere else. Richard King used to stay at the Menger."

"The King Ranch Richard King?"

"Yes. He died there."

"You're *kidding*."

"They had his funeral in the parlor in the 1880s, if I remember correctly. But I can still see the bar—cherry-wood-paneled ceilings and beveled-glass mirrors. They dismantled it during Prohibition but reassembled it when I was a child. I used to love to go in there with Dad and look around. How typical of him to take me to a bar!"

I tell her we saw her old house on Alta. "It looked good," I say. "All fixed up, renovated. One of the best-looking houses in Alamo Heights."

Her mood clouds. "I'm glad you did not have my childhood."

"Thanks to you."

The cloud lifts a little. "I did a good job, didn't I?"

I realize that parents are never too old to be reassured. "You did a *great* job."

She asks when Ross and I are going to Kingsville.

"Day after tomorrow."

"Say hello to Texas A&I for me."

I promise I will, then I tell her I love her and say goodnight.

Ross and I hit the sack, agreeing to sleep in tomorrow. This *is* a vacation. Spring break. Easter week. Time for a little rest and renewal.

My head sinks into the soft Menger pillow. "Goodnight, Ross. I love you."

"I love you, too," he says, sleepy, then, after a pause, "Thanks for doing this, Mom."

"Thank *you*, darling boy."

I lie awake for a while in this cavernous room, in the hotel my grandfather air-conditioned, in the city where my mother was born, where her mother and father first met and married, where their parents settled on the banks of the San Antonio River, and I listen to my own child sleeping in the bed next to mine. For better or worse, his life has been shaped by the choices I've made, just as mine has been shaped by my mother's choices, and hers by her parents', and so on back in time.

"We carry our ancestors within us," the writer Terry Tempest Williams once told me when I was a Nonfiction Fellow at Bread Loaf Writers' Conference.

I didn't understand what she meant. Now I do. Our lives encircle the generations before us, like rings on a tree.

Monday, April 13, 1998

Trip budget: **$345.59**

Hard Rock T-shirt: −$14.01 (Visa)
Alamo IMAX: −$14.00 (Visa)
Anaqua Grill plus tip: −$18.01 (Visa)
Spurs program: −$5.00 (cash)
Mango ice cream: −$8.00 (Visa)

Balance remaining: **$286.57**

CHAPTER SEVENTEEN

The Menger

I wake up early, worried about Echo Lake. My interview is today at four o'clock. I need to review the notes in my journal. Most of all, I need coffee, but our hotel room—for all its comfort and space—does not have a coffee maker. I slip into the bathroom and yesterday's clothes.

Ross is still sleeping. His mouth twitches into a smile. His dream must be happy, the game last night, maybe, the Spurs "growing a pair," as he put it. Swarming the Lakers. Great snowballs of bodies rolling toward the high-dollar seats.

I leave him alone with his happy dream, make sure the door locks behind me, and take the elevator down to the lobby overlooking the garden where Mom sat with Granddaddy when he finished his day's work on the hotel's air-conditioning job. I look at the Menger bar, empty at this early hour. She was right, it's a beauty—beamed wooden ceilings and beveled-glass mirrors. Antique tables and chairs. Yes, I can see Richard King making cattle deals here. King, who founded the ranch that founded the town—Kingsville—where my mother found her freedom. I imagine her sitting here in the bar—a freckled tomboy, as I was—sitting across from her father and sipping a Coke.

How typical of Daddy to take me to a bar!

I'm struck again how our lives are shaped by our parents' choices. Mom chose to move us to Kingsville and build her own life, even though her father didn't think she deserved one. I chose to quit writing. Ross is still angry at me, but isn't he doing a similar thing, quitting school a year early? And I don't even know why. I don't know if I'll ever know.

Another thought arrives on the crest of a small wave of guilt—*maybe the two are related*. I remember something a friend of mine told me. Her husband was fired when their son was a teen. The son's grades went to hell. He didn't give a shit about school, because, as their family therapist told them, he'd internalized his father's feelings of failure.

I wonder if Ross has internalized mine.

Coffee, I think, pushing parental guilt from my mind. I walk past the shops in the lobby—*Silver Spur, Posters on the Plaza*. There *has* to be a coffee pot somewhere. I peek in one of the parlors—no coffee pot, but a wonderful painting of a woman standing triumphantly over the calf she's just roped. My kind of woman. Momzilla. The landscape in the painting looks like the King Ranch, and maybe it is. I feel pulled back in time. San Antonio is the landscape of my mother's childhood, but tomorrow, after Ross and I visit Austin, I'll return to Kingsville, the landscape of mine.

I swear I smell coffee. Like a heat-seeking missile, I move through the Menger's Victorian lobby (this place has a number of lobbies)—three stories high with a leaded-glass skylight and eight

Corinthian columns festooned with gold modillions and garlands. I cross the mosaic floor to the foyer outside the Colonial Dining Room Restaurant and—*hallelujah!*—there's a silver coffee pot. I take two Styrofoam cups, both for me because Ross doesn't drink coffee. And when Ross was a baby, I dreamed about having the leisure to drink a second cup of coffee. At the time, it seemed like an unattainable dream—like an unbroken night's sleep. People told me, "They grow up so fast. He'll be grown in a minute. Before you know it, he'll be leaving home," but I didn't believe them. I fill both cups. The coffee comes out dark as crude oil. Black gold.

On the elevator, riding up to our room, I glance at myself in the stainless-steel panel to see how scuzzy I look (pretty scuzzy) and I remember a scene in my dissertation—a novel—where my heroine, Roz, checks out how she looks in the very same way. But what hits me—sharp, sudden, a *pang*—is how happy I felt when I wrote that book. The sheer damn joy of creating. How odd that this spark, this bit of bliss recollected, would strike me today when I'm taking the Echo Lake job. The elevator doors slide open and I step off, glancing over my shoulder, as if I've left something important behind.

Balancing one coffee cup stacked on top of the other, I let myself back into our room. Ross is still zonked out. I open the balcony's sliding glass doors, step into the cool morning air, sit and prop my feet up on the wrought-iron table, pry the lid off my first cup of coffee, take a sip. The breeze lifts the Texas flag on the flagpole.

Ross wakes around ten, takes a long shower, and emerges from our baronial bathroom in his San Antonio Hard Rock Café T-shirt and his seersucker shorts. "Could we walk through the Alamo one more time?"

We do. He lingers. I let him.

"Breakfast?" I ask as we walk back to the Menger.

"Nah," he says. "Let's grab an early lunch on our way to Austin."

We check out of this historic hotel, so rich in our family history, and throw our stuff in the car. After paying for parking, we drive to I-37, which will take us to I-35, which will take us to Austin.

Ross smiles happily as we pass the Alamodome. "We'll always have San Antonio, Mom."

Tuesday, April 14, 1998

Trip budget:	**$286.57**
Menger parking:	−$6.00 (Visa)
Balance remaining:	**$280.57**

CHAPTER EIGHTEEN

The National Wildflower Research Center

"You and Mimaw have talked so often about bluebonnets in Texas, and there they are." Ross is leaning on the wall of the observation tower—a strange limestone spiral that resembles a ruin—looking out at the Wildflower Meadow. Bluebonnets under a stonewashed blue sky.

I hear my mother's voice:

I remember running up to my knees in the bluebonnets when I was a little kid, picking as many as I could because I took them home and played with them.

I remember the scene in *The Trip to Bountiful*—a young mother chasing her son, a young boy, through a field of bluebonnets—the film's opening sequence, a film about a woman who returns to the small town where she came of age, as I will tomorrow.

Ross reads the sign: "*Lupinus subcarnosus*. A wild prairie flower belonging to the pea family. "

"I didn't know that," I say.

He gives me that *duh* look and points to the peas hanging off the plant.

"Ah." I look more closely at the stalk of bonnet-shaped flowers, blue with white centers.

He pulls out the guide to the Wildflower Center and reads aloud as we walk through the gardens: "'The Hill Country is part of the Edwards Plateau and stretches west across the center of the state as far as Big Bend. In addition to its own unique ecological features, it's the southern extent of the Midwestern Prairies, the eastern edge of the Chihuahuan Desert, the northern extent of the Tamaulipan Thornscrub, and the western edge of the Southeastern Woodlands.'" He slides the guide back in his pocket. "Cool," he says. "The intersection of five ecosystems."

"Amazing," I say, mesmerized by the beds of pink evening primrose, red autumn sage, yellow damianita, lanceleaf coreopsis, mealy blue sage, blackfoot daisy. I hunker down to study the striped purple center of a pale-pink foxglove.

Once, when Anne was a young girl—eleven or twelve—she was fascinated by the different colors and designs of the phlox that grew wild at our farm in north Florida, and she exclaimed, "Whoever invented phlox must have had a wonderful time!"

When I was her age, if someone had told me that flowers would make me this happy, I would've spat on the ground through the gap between my front teeth. But standing here now, surrounded by flowers, I understand why Lady Bird Johnson said in her welcoming message that beauty is one of our deepest needs. I agree—a necessity, not a luxury. I understand why we send flowers to cele-brate birthdays, weddings, and opening nights. I understand why we send flowers to tell people we love them or to cheer those who suffer from sickness or loss. Looking at these beds of bright flow-ers, I feel my own losses lessen. I understand why, for one Dharma talk, the Buddha simply held up a flower.

"You can't avoid Paradise, you can only avoid seeing it," one of my favorite Zen teachers, Joko Beck, said. And we do. We get so caught up in our lives that we miss the *thisness*. A rose is a rose is a rose. I gaze out at the gardens. This. Flowers. Sky. Sun.

I look up at Ross, waiting patiently for me. "This can't be much fun for you," I say, standing.

He slings his arm over my shoulder. "I'm enjoying you enjoy-ing the flowers."

I feel myself falling more deeply in love with this boy. This young man. A Ross is a Ross is a Ross. This. Flowers. Sky. Son.

Further on down the path, Ross cracks up laughing at a tall skinny sign:

DO NOT
PICK
TWIST OFF
SEVER
CUT
CLIP
SNIP
SNAP OFF
PLUCK

PULL

PINCH OFF

BEND

CRUSH

PARE

BREAK

CLEAVE

DIVIDE

TOUCH

TAKE

STEAL

BORROW

REMOVE

STOMP ON

ROLL OVER

MASH

SMASH

SMUSH

FROWN UPON

OR OTHERWISE HARM

THE PROTECTED NATIVE PLANTS.

THANKS!

I smile as I read it. "Not bad advice for bringing up children, either."

Ross chuckles. "Really."

If our purpose as people is to "bring forth the flower of our own life," as another Zen master said, our purpose as parents is to bring forth the flower of our children's lives. Help them become who they are, not who we want them to be.

I look at Ross across a bed of square-bud primrose—the same bright gold as the words *HARD ROCK* on his T-shirt—and I wonder if I'm a good enough parent to do that.

Maybe not, but it seems important to try.

Tuesday, April 14, 1998

Trip budget:	**$280.57**
Adobe Café/lunch:	−$17.40
Wildflower Center:	−$5.25 (cash)
Gifts/Mom/Anne:	−$7.25 (Visa)
Balance remaining:	**$250.67**

CHAPTER NINETEEN

Austin

"Austin was a vast savannah—a softly undulating expanse of grass punctuated with oaks," says our pamphlet guide to the Wildflower Center. Less than two centuries later, the city sprawls across the fragile hill country like a lava flow of concrete. It's grown like a teen—fast, gangly, out of control. In the last decade, the population has increased by two hundred thousand and is now pushing one million if you count the ticky-tacky houses, malls, and motels that Ross and I are passing as we drive north toward this otherwise supercool city. Air quality reportedly sucks in the summer, and I can believe it—a haze hangs over it now, and it's only mid-April.

Entering Austin feels like re-entering time. I have to call Echo Lake and talk to Doug Mankoff at four. And I realize with a wave of what feels like nostalgia that it's already Tuesday. We left Tallahassee on Friday and we'll be back this Friday.

"Our trip is half over," I tell Ross.

He laughs and shoots me that *lighten up* look. "There's still half to go."

"That age-old debate—half full or half empty."

He smiles. "You haven't even seen Kingsville."

Ross wants to see the George Washington Carver Museum, a modest collection of homespun displays we find housed in the front room of Austin's first public library building. I'm fascinated and saddened by Carver's childhood. Shortly after he was born, his father was killed in an accident, and his mother was kidnapped by Night Riders. He was reared by Susan and Moses Carver, who owned him until slavery was abolished in 1865.

But Ross, my budding biologist, is absorbed by Carver's contributions to agriculture and science. I don't want to rush him—he didn't rush me at the Wildflower Center. Still, I have to call Echo Lake in an hour, and I figure the best place to find an indoor pay phone is the Capitol building, which we find across the Colorado River in the heart of downtown.

"Home of Governor George Walker Bush," I say, parking the Mystique near the Governor's Mansion. "Some people say he'll be president someday."

We both guffaw.

We walk up the Easter-green lawn to the Capitol building. I can't help laughing when I see it up close.

Ross looks at me. "What?"

"Well, it's *pink*." I consult our guidebook. "Yep, pink granite from Granite Mountain near Marble Falls. A railroad had to be built to transport it to Austin. It took sixty-two Scottish stone cutters working with convicts to build it."

Ross mimics Scottie's Scottish accent on *Star Trek*. "I can't do it, Cap'n."

"It's the biggest state capitol in the country, second only in size to the US Capitol, but seven feet taller."

"Well, of *course*." He chuckles, studying a cannon out front.

I pull out the camera.

"No, Mom," he warns.

"Why not?"

"We'll look like some dorky tourists."

"We *are* dorky tourists."

He scowls and leans on the cannon like he's aiming it at me.

I snap the picture. "What is it with you?"

"I'm of the whole Africa thing where a picture steals your soul." He snatches the camera. "So I'll take the pictures."

We enter the cool granite building and cross the inlaid terrazzo floor commemorating the battles for Texas Independence. Ross slows down to remember the Alamo. When we reach the rotunda, he photographs the dome with the gold Lone Star at the center. We can see people walking around the base of the dome, like visitors at the whispering gallery at St. Paul's Cathedral in London.

Ross points up. "I want to take a picture from there."

"Help me find a pay phone first."

We walk down a long marble hallway to a nice quiet corner with pay phones and a copy machine.

"Perfect," I say. "Go take your picture." Ross heads for the rotunda. "But don't fall."

He mugs disappointment. "You *never* let me have any fun."

I pull my journal out of my purse and find Echo Lake's number. The clock over the copy machine says four o'clock. This is it, I think, my new career—literary consultant for a rising-star production company in LA.

I call collect, as Kelly instructed. Sure enough, she answers and accepts the charges. We chat for a couple of minutes, catching up on our lives, then she asks me to hold for Doug Mankoff. A moment later he comes on the phone and says without taking a breath, "Yes, I've thought about hiring you, and I don't have the budget to pay what you're worth."

A compliment and a kiss-off. I realize the interview's over. *This won't hurt, did it?*

Ross saunters up, smiling, the camera slung over his shoulder.

"Well," I say to Doug Mankoff, "keep me in mind."

Ross face falls—*oh, shit.*

I hang up.

"You didn't get it?"

"No," I say, a bit stunned. "He said he couldn't pay what I'm worth."

Ross looks at me, his face a mix of concern and compassion. He wasn't crazy about the Echo Lake option, but it never crossed his mind—or mine—that it wouldn't be offered. "You okay?" he asks.

"Sure," I say, not sure at all.

"Geez, Mom, what will you do?"

"Suck it up and go back to teaching when my sabbatical's over."

"Well, you *are* a great teacher."

I pat his cheek. "And you're a great son."

"There are times when you feel like your luck has run out, when the cup isn't half full or half empty—it's chipped, and you break a tooth," as comedienne Janeane Garofalo says. That's how I feel standing here at the pay phone calling hotels. Rooms downtown are more than a hundred a night. No one has a state rate. I'm down to my last quarter and dime.

Ross stands by, silent, not sure what to say.

I look through our guidebook again for hotels I haven't called yet, and I see that the Austin Youth Hostel rents rooms for twenty-eight bucks a night.

Ross brightens. "Go for it."

I slide the coins in the slot and punch in the number.

A woman answers. "Austin's Youth Hostel, Sam speaking." When I ask for a room, she says, "Oh, sorry. We only have one, and it's booked for the night."

I look at Ross, shake my head.

"Hang on," Sam says. I hear her talking to someone. She comes back on the line. "You're not gonna believe this—the room just opened up."

The Park Inn taught us a valuable lesson—*Look before you sleep*. So Ross and I drive out to the hostel, a former boathouse overlooking the Colorado River.

"Howdy," Sam greets us warmly. "Welcome to Austin." She's about my age with long, unruly, prematurely gray hair, baggy jeans, and a billowing white peasant shirt. She shows us our prospective room, no frills but fine—a double bed and two bunk beds.

"I'll sleep here." Ross slaps the bottom bunk. It sloshes.

"Waterbed mattress," Sam says.

"Cool!" Ross exclaims.

I smile at Sam. "Looks like we'll take it."

We follow her to the front desk and pay for the room now since we'll be leaving for Kingsville first thing in the morning.

Ross asks the best way to see Austin's bats.

"Oh, yeah," Sam says, "you'll want to do that. They fly out from under the Congress Avenue Bridge around sunset, so you've got plenty of time. Have dinner at TGI Fridays. It's kinda pricey, but their deck looks right out on the bridge." She hands back my Visa card. "And don't miss Barton Springs. The city's soul," she says proudly. "The Native Americans who settled here believed that the springs have healing spiritual powers."

"Good," Ross says, glancing at me.

After a couple of wrong turns, we find Barton Springs, but they're closed, the chain-link fence locked up tight. A sign says the swimming hole is still open.

"When God closes a spring, he opens a swimming hole," I say.

Ross pats my back. "Remember that, Mom."

We walk down a long, hot, dusty trail dotted with pink evening primrose. The sound of laughing and splashing wafts our way from the swimming hole up ahead where a half-dozen guys about Ross's age are cannonballing off the low limestone cliffs. They hoot as they hit the water.

"I'm going in," Ross announces.

"In your clothes?"

"They'll be dry by the time we get back to the car." He kicks off his shoes and pulls off his socks and his T-shirt and tosses them to me. And raising his hands over his head, he slowly wades into the water until it's up to the waist of his seersucker shorts, then he dives in and swims.

I kick off my sandals and wade. The water is cold, and the bottom is rocky. I open my hands like a hymnal and scoop water over my face, hoping for healing spiritual power. It cools me, soothes.

The guys take turns leaping into the water, but Ross swims off by himself. A lonely tableau, but maybe it isn't. This spring he wrote an essay describing himself: "When I am in a new group of people, I am fairly shy. I normally hang back until I get a feeling of where I fit in and then act normally."

I give him space. The last thing he needs around a group of new guys is being seen with his mother. I sit out of sight on a log where I can see Ross through the trees, just in case he starts drowning. But he doesn't talk to the others. He swims, alone.

Alone. The way he feels at Maclay, though I still don't understand why.

One of the guys cannonballs, splashing his friends. Their laughter echoes off the limestone cliffs.

Echo.

Echo Lake.

Kiss that one goodbye.

I feel a flurry of panic—what the hell *will* I do? I'm so burned out I don't want to go back to teaching. I have no idea which way my life's heading. The future feels like a void, and I feel a familiar impulse to fill it, so I pull a pen and my journal out of my purse to brainstorm my options on paper. But when I open my journal I see a quotation from one of my favorite Buddhist teachers and writers, Pema Chödrön:

> The instruction is to stop. Do something unfamiliar. Do anything besides rushing off in the same old direction, up to the same old tricks. The instruction is not to solve the problem but instead to use it as a question about how to let this very situation wake us up further . . . Maybe the most important teaching is to lighten up and relax.

What Ross has been saying the whole trip.

When we pay attention, our children teach us.

I put the pen and journal away and sit still, breathing deeply. I feel the rough bark of the log through the seat of my jeans. I smell the dust in the air. I hear the guys splashing and shouting. I watch Ross watching them.

He seems deep in thought, then he nods as if he's reached some realization. He dives and swims a stretch underwater and breaches, shaking his head and spraying a pinwheel of water that catches the afternoon sun.

Our skinny undergraduate waiter at TGI Fridays seats us at a table out on the deck overlooking the Congress Avenue Bridge. He's a budding aficionado about free-tailed bats. "Each March they migrate from Central Mexico to roost sites located here in the Southwest," he says, handing us menus. "Three-quarters of a million pregnant females nest under the Congress Avenue Bridge every year. Each has one pup. By November the babies are old enough to hitch a ride south with the group."

I open my menu. "That's a buttload of bats."

The waiter smiles proudly. "Largest urban bat population in North America."

"Largest and grandest," I say, but he's too young to get it.

"They eat anywhere from ten thousand to thirty thousand pounds of insects a night. That's a buttload of *bugs*."

"Why free-tailed?" Ross asks.

"Their tail extends beyond the tail membrane. They're cool to look at—a wingspan of up to twelve inches. Large ears, sharp teeth."

I grimace. "Tell me they won't get too close."

"They don't get tangled up in your hair, if that's what you're thinking. And they aren't really blind."

"So 'blind as a bat' is pure guano."

"Yep," he says. "They see better than we do at dusk, but then they need some help in the dark so they use—"

"Echolocation," Ross finishes for him.

"Bat radar," I add.

"Right," says the waiter. "To know what's in their path. Size, shape, distance, direction."

We order burgers, fries, Cokes. The waiter goes off to get them.

I gaze at the bridge, a graceful series of arches supporting the bypass spanning Town Lake. The sun hovers over the bridge. "I could use a little echolocation."

Ross's face catches the last golden light. "Because Echo Lake rejected you?"

"Yeah. I guess I feel a bit . . . lost."

"Me, too," he says.

"Do you?" I'm surprised he's so open.

He shakes salt in the palm of his hand and tastes it with the tip of his tongue. "It's like I told you before—about the Demented Ultimate Freaks. I get to go fun places and do fun things with the FSU guys. You know, hang out with college kids, but I haven't been home on weekends to party with my friends at Maclay, and no one at FSU is going to invite me along for spring break. And my friends are all at Mexico Beach."

I feel a flash of guilt that he's spending spring break with me. "You could have gone with them."

"Mom," he says, "they didn't invite me."

"Oh, *sweetheart*." Now I understand why he's been feeling so blue—not just blue but *abandoned*. "Are you okay?"

He looks out at the bridge. "Actually, I feel like ass, but it's my own fault. Every time they ask what I'm doing on the weekend, I say I'm playing Ultimate with FSU—*Hey, look at me, they're letting me play in college*—like I'm better than they are. They blew me off, yes, but I blew them off first." He takes a glug of his water and sets down the glass. "And I don't think it was all of the guys. There's this one kid hates my guts."

"Which kid?" My tone betrays that I'd cheerfully kill him.

"It doesn't matter. He's a year older but hangs out with sophomores. I'll crack a joke, and everyone will be laughing, and he'll look at me like I suck and say, 'That's really funny, Ross.'"

"What an asshole!"

"Oh, yeah," Ross says, then he smiles, nice and wicked. "But I got him back. A bunch of us went to see *The Big Lebowski*. This kid hated the film. So after the movie he makes this pronouncement, 'Anyone who likes *The Big Lebowski* does not have a penis.' Just then Risher walks up and has no idea what this kid just said, and he says he loved *The Big Lebowski*. Everyone laughs. Then Tim walks up—no idea, either—and says *he* loved *The Big Lebowski*. Everyone cracks up. So I look down at my crotch and say, 'Shit! There it goes!'"

I laugh.

So does Ross. "Pissed him off big time, but, hey, it was worth it."

The waiter sets down our burgers and fries. "Anything else?"

I glance at the bridge. The sun's long gone now. "Tell the frickin' bats to come out."

"I'll do that," he says, droll, and goes.

Ross smothers his French fries with ketchup. "Today, watching those guys at the springs, I kind of realized, like, I mean, I've devoted all my time to playing Ultimate at FSU, but I'm a high-school student and I have to start acting like one. You know, figure out where I belong."

"Oh, baby, I know the feeling. Believe me, I know." It's another one of those odd intersections, like having the same escape fantasy. We're facing the same dilemma—how to find our place in the world—and we have to create ways to solve it, as Kierkegaard says, or we shrink our Self and our freedom. I eat a few French fries, the salt mixing with the sweet taste of the ketchup. The evening air feels soft on my face. Town Lake has turned a deep blue. "Did you read Kierkegaard for your philosophy panel this year at Maclay?"

"No, just Spinoza and Nietzsche."

I remember the cardboard nameplate he made for himself— FRIEDRICH NIETZSCHE (BUT YOU CAN CALL ME FRED). I keep it on my desk.

"Why?" He takes a big bite of burger.

"Kierkegaard says freedom comes from confronting and overcoming situations that cause anxiety, fear."

Ross sets down his burger. "Like what?"

"Like finding our place in the world. I guess everyone faces that at some point. I know Mom did in Corpus."

"How so?"

"How 'bout I tell you later, so we don't miss the bats?"

"Tell me now."

I nod. "After the Zane Grey book episode, Granddaddy went crazy."

"Crazier."

"Right. Threatened to take it out on Mamaw, who hid out at our house all hopped up on drugs."

She stayed in that back bedroom where Patty slept. Oh, I had to put up with her nutty as a fruitcake. Just when you thought she'd pass out, she'd reel down the hall and stagger into the kitchen in her long housecoat trying to be the grand lady. Then she'd collapse at the table. She wouldn't admit what was the matter, so I asked her point blank, "Why do you let him do this to you? Why don't you leave him?" She lashed out, "I am Mrs. A. W. Morgan! I am Mrs. A. W. Morgan!" And I said, "Who is that?" She just crumpled. "Nobody," she said.

"That's so sad," Ross says.
"Mom said so, too."

You grow up with this woman, and she's your mother, and she begins to melt like a snowman. Then Granddaddy would call me on the phone at midnight and threaten to kill me. I mean, "I'm gonna come out there and blow your goddamn head off—and your kids'." I fully expected we would get shot if we stayed in Corpus. I knew at some point he'd do it—"blow you and your goddamn kids' brains out." I felt like I was drowning. When your own mother goes cuckoo. They were both cuckoo. She stood in the living room in front of the heater—it was a cold night—and I was trying to reason with her, and she said, "Well, you'll get yours." And I said, "Listen, I've had it since I was ten years old, and I'm leaving." That's when I decided I couldn't take anymore. I had to get out of Corpus.

"So that spring Mom finished her AA degree, then she hit a big snag—the only four-year program in town was the University of Corpus Christi. Private. Very pricey. She knew it would take forever to scrape up the money to finish. And it was run by the Baptists."

"Hoo boy." Ross laughs, knowing what a liberal she is.

"She took one class that summer—History of the South, Baptist slant."

"Save your Confederate money, the South will rise again."

"Yes, exactly. She hated it. But a classmate mentioned a cheap little college over in Kingsville—Texas A&I—that only charged sixty dollars tuition for a full-time semester. If we moved there, Mom could finish her bachelor's degree in two years."

"That's when you moved."

"No, we couldn't."

"Why?"

"Granddaddy repo'd the car."

Ross tosses his napkin on the table.

"Mom was stuck. Couldn't go, couldn't stay."

"But you did move to Kingsville."

"Thanks to Aunt Patty. She was fed up with Granddaddy bullying Mom. She told Mom she was buying a new car and she'd give her the old one."

"Cool!"

"But Mom wouldn't take it."

Ross looks at me—*not take a car?*

"She didn't think she could pay for repairs—that's how tight money was—but Aunt Patty wouldn't take no for an answer. She sold Mom her old car for a dollar."

It was a humpy old Plymouth. A stumpy little car. Really ugly as hell. But Dad couldn't take it away.

"Mom said she was driving out Ocean Drive, taking us to swim at UCC's pool, when she looked down at the Plymouth's steering wheel and realized, really realized, that she could move us to Kingsville. I remember when we got to the pool, I was bobbing around in the deep end, and I saw my mother step up on the diving board in her white bathing suit. She stood there a moment, gazing at something off in the distance—her future, perhaps—then she bent down like she was touching her toes, pressed the palms of her hands flat on the board, and her body unfolded like a jackknife. A perfect handstand. And she walked on her hands the length of the diving board, paused at the end, her back straight, her toes pointed toward the blue Texas sky, and she flipped into the water, barely making a ripple."

Ross leans back, smiling. "Wow."

"That's what I thought. I mean, my *mother*? I didn't know she could do shit like that."

"Momzilla," Ross says.

"She really was."

The sky is lavender now. A bat darts past the deck.

"I saw one!" I shout, idiotic.

We see a few more wheeling into the darkness, but in the end the bats are a fizzle. We can't see them when they fly out from under the bridge. We can only see, in the distance, in the twilight, a cloud of bats that looks more like smoke.

"It's a temperature issue," our waiter explains when I pay our bill. "By the time it was right for the bats to come out, it was too dark to see them."

"Now you tell us," I kid, but I leave the best tip I can. We've hogged his table all evening.

Ross and I say goodnight and walk back to the car and head for the Austin Youth Hostel, the small black Mystique wheeling into the darkness.

Tuesday, April 14, 1998

Trip budget: **$250.67**

Pay phone: −$1.75 (cash)
Youth Hostel: −$40.00 (Visa)
TGI Fridays   −$15.00 (Visa)
HEB (cereal/milk):   −$6.29 (cash)

Balance remaining: **$187.63**

PART THREE

CHAPTER TWENTY

Highway 77 to Kingsville

Wednesday, April 15, 1998

I came of age in South Texas, in a landscape as flat as my chest at the time. I came of age in a cow town called Kingsville, complete with all the clichés—oil wells, rattlesnakes, tumbleweeds, vast horizons—and a two-block downtown that ended at the Texas Theater, where tiles drifted down from the ceiling and *las cucarachas* raced across the backs of the cracked red-leather seats during movies and the soft drink of choice was called Suicide.

That is the town I remember, but now, heading south on I-37, Ross sleeping beside me, I start to wonder if anything there will be the same. A flurry of worries. What if it's changed as much as Ann said? What if it alters what I remember?

"What are we without our memories?" Dr. Lawhorn said sadly to me when he diagnosed my mother's dementia.

Second only to losing Ross and my mother, losing my memories scares me the most.

I exit onto Highway 77, the last stretch of highway to Kingsville, and the landscape is as stark as I remember. Flat, bleak farmland. Dirt so black it looks purple. A farmhouse every few miles. The only thing that's changed is the crop—soybeans now. When I was a girl, it was cotton.

Ross stirs in the passenger seat. When he finally surfaces, he stares out the window like someone from Oz who just woke up in Kansas.

"I warned you this stretch was butt-ugly."

"Jesus," he says, "I thought you were joking."

"No. I had the same stricken look when Mom drove us to Kingsville in the aqua-blue Plymouth. I was ten, slumped down in the back seat, staring at rows of picked-over cotton and horsehead pumps that looked like bloodsucking insects."

"Yeah," Ross says as we pass one now. "I can see the proboscis."

"It was August 1961. Hot, Jesus God, it was hot. Heat waves rising off of the highway. The car windows rolled down. I remember the hot wind whipping my face and the feel of grit in my teeth from the dirt blowing off the cotton fields. And I remember how heartbroken and angry I was at my mother for making us move. Patty was angry, too. Both of us were boo-hooing. But Mom kept on driving, lips tight, that look that she'd get, maybe all mothers get when they're doing something they know makes their children unhappy."

Ross nods knowingly. "But she had to do it."

"I know that now. But back then I hated her for taking me away from my neighborhood friends and Jeff and Jon and Aunt Patty and Hansie, our dachshund. We couldn't have pets in the student apartment Mom rented for us at Texas A&I, so she had to give him away. I didn't even *like* the damn dog—he was always chewing my toys—but I hated her for giving him up. And she knew it."

Giving up the dog broke my heart, but I had no choice. I had to build a life for myself. But both of you were upset. All kids hate being uprooted. I remember you cried all the way over there, tears down your faces. Y'all were happy little kids back in Corpus. You had your little neighborhood, and you didn't know how bad it was with Mother and Dad. I kept it from you as long as I could. But I was elated. Relieved. Oh, my God, yes, to get away from Daddy. A goddamn raving mean drunk. He's burning in hell somewhere, the things he did to my mother. And the farther I drove the more elated I felt. Going to Kingsville was a form of going to heaven. It felt that way to me, just getting away from there. God knows I didn't have that much money, but that didn't stop me. Hell, no. I felt like I was going to heaven because I was going on with my education. It was the opening of the door to freedom for me, getting out of Corpus, because Dad couldn't touch me. I was on my way to heaven. Going through the Golden Gate. Just getting away. "Forty miles to freedom" was a phrase I used. As you and Patty and I drove down the Chapman Ranch Road to Highway 77, we were going to our highway to freedom.

I point out where Highway 77 intersects with the Chapman Ranch Road. "That's where Mom turned south for these last six miles to Kingsville." We're just north of Bishop, home of the Celanese chemical plant. "Well, *that* hasn't changed," I say as we drive past the smokestacks still belching white smoke. "I remember that sicky-sweet smell. Winter mornings we'd open the door, and if we smelled it we knew a norther was coming."

"A norther?" Ross asks.

"A cold front from the north. Texans call the bad ones 'blue northers.' They hit so hard and fast temperatures can drop fifty degrees in less than an hour. And you see them coming—a steel-blue bank of clouds on the horizon of an otherwise harmless blue sky. That's how I came to think of Granddaddy—our blue norther. We'd moved forty miles south of Corpus, but he was still out there on the horizon."

I slow down as we drive through Bishop—still butt-ugly, too.

Ross slips off his shoe and scratches his foot. That sour-mash smell of ripe socks fills the car. We left the Youth Hostel so early, he didn't shower. "After you moved, did you see him and Mamaw again?"

"We had to go back to Corpus some weekends because Mamaw's drug addiction was getting worse. I remember her nightstand, covered with amber plastic pill bottles—her own little Celanese plant."

It's late morning, almost eleven, when we see a small gray frame building: KINGSVILLE VISITOR CENTER.

"That wasn't here when I was a girl." I pull in and park in front.

Ross leans back and closes his eyes. "I'll wait here while you check it out."

Inside, a tall, silver-haired man in a western shirt and string tie sits behind a counter stacked with brochures about the King Ranch and a basket of I (HEART) KINGSVILLE bumper stickers. The tail of the G in KINGSVILLE is shaped like a spur.

"Welcome to Kingsville," he says, a Chamber-of-Commerce smile on his face.

I tell him I'm here with my son.

"Then you'll have to take him to King's Inn and the King Ranch."

"King's Inn is still open?" I ask, amazed.

"Best Gulf shrimp in the world."

"I remember the wonderful shrimp. I grew up here."

"No kidding," he says, his smile getting warmer.

"No kidding."

He hands me a King Ranch brochure.

"Can you still drive out the Loop Road?"

"No, it's closed off to cars, but you can take a bus tour. The last one's at three. And don't miss downtown. JB Ragland Mercantile Building is on the National Register."

"Ragland's!" I remember it well.

"It's the King Ranch Saddle Shop now."

"Ah." Things *have* changed.

"Harrel's Pharmacy is also historic."

I laugh. "You have no idea."

He looks at me curiously.

I straighten my face. "Is Nicky Harrel still there?"

"Nicky, Jr.'s the pharmacist now. Since his daddy retired."

I smile. Nicky, Jr. My first kiss.

I've forgotten how far it is out to King's Inn—way the hell out Highway 628 to Loyola Beach. Miles of south Texas scrub—grass and lanceleaf coreopsis and prickly-pear cactus in pale-yellow bloom. The long drive is burning up valuable time, but if King's Inn hasn't changed, it'll be worth it. "They served the biggest Gulf shrimp I've seen in my life."

"Good," Ross says. "I'm *starving*."

"We only ate there a few times. Mostly, if we went out at all, Mom took us to this great Tex-Mex place, El Jardin. When she could afford it."

"Let's go there for dinner."

"Absolutely—if it's still there." I stop for five wild turkeys crossing the road. "But Mom was so happy living in Kingsville, she never felt poor even though money was tight. 'We're rich, we just don't have any money.' That was her mantra."

"Sort of like us."

"Sort of," I smile, realizing he's saying we're rich anyway. He's more evolved about money than I am. Sometimes he's more evolved about *life*. He keeps a page from my Little Zen Calendar next to his bed, a quotation from Samuel Johnson: "When making your choice in life, do not forget to live." "But you and I have way more money than Mom did back then. It was a miracle she made ends meet."

"How'd she do it?"

"Made her own clothes. Taught Patty and me to make ours. She built her own bookshelves. Rewired the vacuum cleaner."

"The hell it won't fit, give me a bigger hammer!" Ross says, having heard it many times.

"Oh, yeah. She cooked big pots of pinto beans for a dollar. She'd buy the dried beans, soak them overnight, and simmer them the next day with salt, chili powder, and an onion as big as your fist. They were some of the world's greatest soul food. Delicious—but deadly."

Ross snickers.

"We'd eat pinto beans every night for a week."

The last wild turkey lurches into the scrub. I drive on. "You know the campfire scene in *Blazing Saddles*?"

"Mom, it's a classic."

"That's what *our* dinners were like. And when we went out in public—let's just say we should've been registered as lethal weapons."

"Like the pillows at the Park Inn."

"Well, a gas, not a solid."

Ross cracks up.

"We had to find ways to cope. Patty backed up to the air return vent at King High. She'd stand there talking to friends and farting like crazy, but nobody knew it."

"Except the people on the other end of the vent."

I laugh so hard the Mystique swerves slightly.

Ross smiles. "So how did *you* cope?"

"Ann and I were inseparable buddies, so whenever I felt a fart coming on, I'd ask her to cover, and she'd cough as loud as she could."

He shakes his head. "You crazy kids."

And he doesn't know the half of it yet.

We share the sample platter at King's Inn—frog legs, crab cakes, scallops, fish, oysters, and yes, the biggest shrimp Ross has seen in his life.

I confess that I'm nervous about seeing Kingsville again.

Ross stares at me across a plate of thick-sliced tomatoes. *Wuss. Weenie.* "That's ridiculous, Mom."

"Remember what Ann said when we left New Orleans?" I smooth a bent corner of my white paper place mat. "Kingsville's changed. It might mess up my memories."

"*Puh!*" He pops a fried oyster into his mouth.

I look out the window at Loyola Beach—green lawns sweeping down to docks and boathouses. Martins dart across sagging gray clouds that look like the underside of a broken-down mattress. As gray as the Gulf at the moment. "Anyway, that's how I feel."

"Scared."

I meet his look. "Yes, a little."

"Then you *have* to see Kingsville."

"Please to explain?"

He bites the head off a jumbo Gulf shrimp. "Remember Kierkegaard, Mom."

Ross disappears while I pay the bill. I find him waiting out front in the driver's seat, the Mystique's engine running. He pushes open the passenger door.

"Mom, *listen*." He cranks up the radio volume, and I hear "Twist and Shout," my all-time favorite oldie, John Lennon cutting loose in a way that blew out his voice and still blows my mind.

I slide in the sun-warmed passenger seat.

Ross turns down the volume. "I'm driving so you can look at stuff, Mom."

"Aw," I say, "that's so thoughtful."

"I'm driving so we don't *die*." He does a good imitation of me rubbernecking and driving and wrecking the car. Complete with sound effects.

I look at him—*ha ha, very funny*. "Well, shake it up, boyo," I say.

Wednesday, April 15, 1998

Trip budget: **$187.63**

Gas: −$16.96 (Visa)
King's Inn/lunch   −$20.88 (Visa)

Balance remaining: **$149.79**

CHAPTER TWENTY-ONE

The King Ranch

"The region was once known as *El Desierto de los Muertos*," the narrator of the King Ranch video tells us—the only people in the small screening room at their Visitor Center—while we wait for the three o'clock tour. "The Desert of the Dead," he translates, his voice deep and melodramatic. "Also known as the Wild Horse Desert, the region was so hot and dry and grass was so sparse, it took twenty acres to feed one head of cattle. There were no live creeks and not many natural basins to catch water from rain. People thought King was crazy."

"Not as crazy as DF Morgan," I whisper to Ross.

He makes a dying bull sound.

The narrator tells us facts I learned at Charles B. Flato Elementary School, but I'm happy Ross is hearing them now: Richard King was a hell-raising Rio Grande steamboat pilot who bought this land in 1853—15,500 acres for $300. He knew it had the first live water 124 miles north of Mexico—the Santa Gertrudis Creek, an oasis shaded by large mesquite trees and cool, sweet water that flowed all year long. He coaxed an entire Mexican town of *vaqueros* to move north and help work the ranch. They're still called the *Kineños*. With their help, he built the King Ranch and developed a world-famous breed of cattle known as the Santa Gertrudis. He owned more than 600,000 acres when he died in 1885.

"At the Menger, according to Mom," I tell Ross.

He raises an eyebrow, impressed.

"Now the King Ranch is 825,000 acres," the narrator's voice thrums. "The size of Rhode Island."

"That's where Brown is," Ross says. As if his mind is made up that he'll go there for college.

When the video ends, we return to the main room and wait for the tour to begin. Ross studies big framed photos of the ranch's claims to fame—Assault, winner of the Triple Crown, and Monkey, the foundation sire of the Santa Gertrudis breed.

"Mom," Ross says, pointing to the photo of Monkey. "How many legs does that bull have?"

I walk over and look closely at Monkey, a massive bull with four legs and a penis the size of Rhode Island. "Um, sweetheart," I say delicately, "that's not a leg."

"Buy land and never sell," says our tour guide, a retired test pilot with gray hair as curly and thick as my father's. "That's been the philosophy of the Kings and the Klebergs. Bigger is better. For six generations, they've been expanding the area that they own. Today it's so big there's a month's difference in the seasons between the northern and southern ends of the ranch. All the fences strung together would stretch from Kingsville to Boston."

"Wow," I say, amazed by that stat.

He's driving us, his only takers, out the Loop Road where Ann and I used to drive when we were Ross's age. For the next hour and a half wc have him and this air-conditioned bus to ourselves—that charmed feeling again.

He tells us about the Main House, still a stark white two-story compound with a central tower that looks like a turret on a medieval castle.

I remember what Mom said:

It was an actual fortress with machine guns on the roof. To protect the house from banditos, that's what people said. Others said King would invite small landowners up to the house, and if they refused to sell him their land, he'd shoot them when they walked away. But who knows? I don't think King killed anyone, but there's no way to know. He got what he wanted one way or the other.

"Any truth to the rumor that King machine-gunned landowners who wouldn't sell him their land?" I ask our tour guide.

He laughs. "No, that never happened."

Ross shoots me a look—*did it?*

I shrug—*dunno.*

Our guide tells us about the crested *caracara* when we pass one perched on top of a telephone pole. "Also called the Mexican Eagle—the national emblem of Mexico—but it's really a falcon."

"Big falcon," I say. It's two feet tall, easy, with long yellow legs and a dark-brown body with a white neck, red face, and a black cap that looks like a really bad hairpiece.

"A tough bird, I'll tell you," our guide adds. "Saw one run off six buzzards over some road kill. Has a high harsh cackle."

"Like you, Mom," Ross says.

Our guide chuckles—a little male bonding.

He tells us about the mesquite tree, which I'm surprised to find out is not native to Texas. "The mesquite you see around here came up from Mexico. You can see it growing all along the course of the old cattle drives. Seedpod's so hard it has to pass through the digestive system of horses or cattle before it can grow."

"Ah," I say. So the tree Ann and I climbed when we bared our souls to each other is linked, like everything else in Kingsville, to cattle culture.

"Mesquite's about all that'll grow around here, except tumble-weed."

Ross lights up. "Will we see tumbleweed?"

"I doubt it," our guide says. "You see them more in the winter and fall when they wither and break off and start rolling around."

"I saw my first tumbleweed here in Kingsville," I tell Ross. "I asked Mom what it was because I'd never seen one in Corpus."

"It'd be so cool to see one!"

"Like the opening sequence of *The Big Lebowski*?"

He smiles at the mention of his favorite movie. "Right. The tumbleweed rolling into LA."

"The song the cowboys are crooning over the credits—'Tumbling Tumbleweeds' I think it's called—Mom used to sing it to me when I was a girl. And she said Granddaddy used to sing it to her."

"Amazing," Ross says.

"You might see one," says our guide, "keep your eyes peeled."

Ross leans forward and scans the wide-open landscape. In his rumpled Hard Rock T-shirt and seersucker shorts, he looks pure Dude.

Our tour guide tells us how things have changed on the Ranch. "At round-up time they still need cowboys with chaps, spurs, and ropes to track the cattle down in the thickets and steer them toward the pens, but the cowboys communicate now by cell phone. They plug their famous Running W branding irons into electrical outlets. Even the Santa Gertrudis is being phased out."

I lean forward. "Why?"

"They've got a new breed—Santa Cruz. Only took eight years to develop because of computers. The Santa Gertrudis took forty—cowboys sitting on fences marking down every trait of the cattle."

"A friend's father was a foreman here at the Ranch," I tell our guide. "And all her brothers were cowboys."

He glances back at me. "Who was her father?"

"Leonard Stiles."

"He still lives here."

I crack up. Okay, I cackle. "You're *kidding*."

"Retired, of course. You'll see him at the end of this tour."

"I used to spend the night at their house."

"We'll drive right past it."

I sit there, slack-jawed.

Ross shoves my shoulder. "See, Mom? Some things haven't changed."

"But first I'm gonna show you one of the greatest quarter horses, the first horse to win the Open World Champion titles from the American Quarter Horse Association and the National Cutting Horse Association in the same year. The youngest horse ever to be inducted into the NCHA Hall of Fame." He pulls over, and there in the shade of a mesquite tree is a swaybacked roan stallion with a white streak that looks like the white spot on his forehead melted and trickled down to his sagging lips.

I blink. "The youngest?"

"Back in the Seventies."

"Ah."

"He's twenty-two now—that's a hundred and eight in horse years—but in his day he was something. Sired *hundreds* of horses. Go say hello to Mr. San Peppy."

Ross and I look at each other—*Mr. San Peppy!*—both of us flashing on the dumb penis joke in *Multiplicity*—*She touched my peppy, Steve!* I don't know who says it first, but both of us do as we get off the bus—"She touched my San Peppy, Steve."

We must be punchy because this sets us off laughing. We stumble toward the hog-wire fence, howling with laughter. Our guide probably thinks we're making fun of poor old Mr. San Peppy. The horse apparently does. He flattens his ears and flares his nostrils at us. We try to stop laughing, but we can't. We're helpless, hanging onto each other, tears streaming down our faces. My ab muscles hurt. Our laughter finally begins to subside, flares up, dies down, and flares up again, until we're too weak to laugh any longer. We straighten our faces and get back on the bus.

"That's the Stileses' house right there." Our guide slows down and points at a sprawling brick ranch house with the same driveway curving to the back door where my mother would drop off Ann Owens and me when we spent the night with Ann Stiles. I can still see Leonard Stiles flanked by his cowboy sons in the morning as they walked away from the house to saddle up for the day, their leather chaps slapping legs that looked like parentheses.

I marvel. "The house looks exactly the same."

But Leonard Stiles doesn't. Thirty-two years later, waiting for us in the weavers' cottage, he looks small and frail in gold wire-rim glasses and a short-sleeved plaid shirt. He must be pushing seventy now, like my mother. And like Mr. San Peppy, he's been put out to pasture.

When I tell Mr. Stiles that I knew his daughter, Ann, back when he was a foreman, he nods politely, but he clearly doesn't remember. And he seems faintly embarrassed to be stuck in this small stucco building telling tourists how saddle blankets were woven, but he hits his proud stride when he shows us his branding-iron collection—a display with over a hundred different brands burned into wood panels.

"What's the origin of the Running W brand?" Ross asks him.

"Unknown," says Mr. Stiles. "Some say it came from all the diamondback rattlesnakes here on the ranch. Others say the winding Santa Gertrudis Creek. Some say the head of a longhorn. Take your pick. Whatever it is, the Running W shape distributes heat better than most other brands. It heals quickly and grows with the cattle.

Before we leave, I ask him what Ann's up to now.

"She and her husband are working a ranch out in Phoenix."

"Any kids?" I ask. The Stiles are a big Catholic family, and I figure Ann has a whole bunch by now.

His face clouds. "No," he says, "no children."

"To real cattlemen, the King Ranch is Eden," our guide continues, driving us back through a part of the ranch far from telephone poles and sprawling ranch houses. "So many important pieces of the cattle industry were invented here, from cattle prods to dipping vats to new breeds of cattle."

"And I bet *they* got patents for them," Ross whispers.

I nod, but I'm barely listening. I'm mesmerized by the land—an unbroken expanse of short grass stretching toward a horizon so distant it's a strip of deep blue. *This* is it. This is what I remember. This is what I loved as a tomboy. Ann Tilton was right, things have changed—they've closed the Loop Road to cars, and cowboys use electric branding irons and cell phones. But this landscape is timeless. I'd forgotten how it *feels* to see this much open space—a sensation of motion as the eye sweeps across it. Vision attempting to take in the vastness.

Vasticity.

I glance at Ross, absorbed in what our tour guide is saying.

I interrupt. "Could we get out and look?"

"Sure," says our guide, surprised that I'd want to. He stops the bus and opens the doors.

Ross raises an eyebrow at me.

"Come on. I want you to see this." He's seen the landscape of my mother's childhood—the San Antonio River and the Texas Hill Country—and now I want him to see the landscape of mine. Not the butt-ugly farmland between Corpus and Kingsville. This. The Wild Horse Desert. The Desert of the Dead. *El Desierto de los Muertos*. Stark. Open. Empty.

He follows me off the bus.

The sun has come out since we started the tour, bleaching the now cloudless sky a pale blue. The color of my mother's eyes. It's so hot in the sun I can smell my flowered rayon shirt scorching as Ross and I stand side by side, surrounded by nothing but grass and mesquite.

After a moment Ross says, "I don't see anything."

And I say, "Exactly."

Wednesday, April 15, 1998

Trip budget: **$149.79**

King Ranch tour: −$14.95 (cash)
King Ranch book: −$6.00 (cash)

Balance remaining: **$128.84**

CHAPTER TWENTY-TWO

Texas A&I

"We're going in!" Ross shouts as we head into town. As if we're taking Kingsville by storm. As if he needs to whip up my courage. And maybe he does. Riding shotgun along Santa Gertrudis Avenue, I feel a little faint-hearted. I don't recognize a damn thing. Then I see it—the main entrance to the Texas A&I campus.

"Good Lord, there it is!"

Ross turns left into the entrance. The sign says it's part of Texas A&M now, and there's a new iron sculpture of two javelinas, but we're driving down the same divided palm-tree-lined drive my mother drove down in our old aqua Plymouth when I was ten. And TEXAS COLLEGE OF ARTS AND INDUSTRIES is still etched in the stucco of the administration building where Ann Owen's mother, Harriette, worked in the registrar's office. Where my mother signed up for classes. Where Ann and I used to roller-skate in and out of the seven big arches. JOIN US HERE FOR THE FUTURE, the sign out front says.

And the past, I think to myself.

Across the street, there's a new bookstore and a new biology building, but between them lies the same sweep of grass that runs to the theater building flanked by two red-tiled ramps that Ann and I loved to fly down on our skates. I recognize the old biology building—one of our favorite haunts—just beyond.

"Pull over, pull over."

Ross does.

"It's still here," I whisper.

He glances at me. "Mom, you okay?"

I realize I have tears in my eyes, and I swipe them away, laughing. "Remember what you said in New Orleans? How Ann and I could entertain ourselves forever in a world all our own?"

"I remember."

"This was it—our own private kingdom. Mom and Harriette gave us the run of the campus. Total freedom. We knew the buildings by heart—and what was inside them. We'd sneak up into the Student Union ballroom and plink around on their grand piano, or cut through the biology building to see the live snakes and dead babies."

Ross's eyelashes rise. "Dead babies?"

"Human fetuses in formaldehyde. You'd never see that kind of thing now with the Right-to-Life movement, but back then we did—two rows of large specimen jars, containing the range of fetal development from a fetus the size of a tadpole to near-full-term Siamese twins."

I tell him about our obsession with Siamese twins, how we'd joke that we were just like them—inseparable buddies. We'd race through the building, our laughter ringing down the long, dingy hallway, but we'd always shut up when we saw them—those two Siamese-twin babies with their heads pressed white against the side of the jar, like the pickled eggs at Grayson's Grocery. We'd stand

there gawking, the smell of formaldehyde mixed with mixed feelings—the fascination and guilt you feel at a freak show.

"Maybe that's why Ann is a doctor."

I cock my head—a connection I never made. "Maybe it is."

Ross drives on around the administration building, and there,
behind the engineering building, I see the student apartments—
rows of yellow-brick duplexes. We drive to the last row and park
in front of the apartment my mother rented thirty-seven years
ago.

I was lucky to have found one that was still available. Rent
was sixty dollars a month. I got one of the nice ones—it was
air-conditioned. Air-conditioned and clean and wonderful. My God, the utility bill was only thirty dollars a month.
That's not bad at all. I liked it because it opened on the pasture—a lovely view of the grass and mesquite trees. God, we
were so poor, but I didn't feel poor. I felt rich for the first
time in my life.

"It hasn't changed, either," I tell Ross. "The same sea-foam-
green door, the small flower bed where I used to keep my pet horny
toad."

Ross snickers.

"The red-tiled porch overlooking that same field of grass and
mesquite where Ann and I used to run like wild horses. We'd run
all the way to a barbed-wire fence on the edge of the King Ranch.
There was a quarter horse there that I loved to pet."

"Mr. San Peppy."

I laugh. "Well, maybe his daddy." I look back at our student
apartment. "The day we moved in I hated this place—and Mom for

bringing us here. I slammed a ladder-back chair on its side across my bedroom door the way I used to do back in Corpus to keep Hansie out."

"Force of habit?" Ross asks.

"No, to punish my mother. Forty miles to freedom, my ass."

You built a barricade even though we didn't have the dog anymore. Oh, yeah, you did this to get even with me. Sure, because it was hard.

"Patty saw the chair and made some snide remark—'Trying to keep out the dog?'—and I burst into tears. Mom came running to see what was wrong, and when she saw that chair a shot of pain crossed her face, but she didn't cave. She said we were staying in Kingsville. This was home now. She suggested I console myself with a book. I locked myself in my room with *The Yearling*."

"Good choice," Ross laughs. "Guaranteed to cheer you right up."

"Oh, yeah. The end nearly finished me off. I flung the book at the wall, pages flapping, and I flung myself on the bed and bawled my eyes out—for Flagg, Jody, Hansie, myself. I cried until I was wrung out, then I ran out of my room and out the front door into that field, ran as fast and far as I could, the grass and sticker burrs brushing my legs, until I got a stitch in my side and had to stop running. I remember standing there, flat chest heaving, surrounded by miles of grass and mesquite, and I realized how cooped up I'd felt in Corpus. And I started to feel free myself."

"Good for you, Mom," Ross says, gazing out at the field.

I tell him how my mother put her books on the bookshelves she built—her badge of honor, proof that she wasn't stupid—then she put white café curtains up in the windows and her own oil paintings up on the walls. "You've seen them—the two Korean orphans, the two clowns playing cards, the black gambler about to roll dice." I tell him how she unrolled our braid rug and shoved our couch, coffee table, and chairs into place.

Her place.

It was exactly the kind of place for a person like me who needed a refuge from the storm. It was safe from my father. Oh, he'd still call. He'd call to call me a whore. "Who are you whoring around with now?" Or he'd threaten to kill me—or you and Patty. "I'm gonna kill your goddamn kids, too." But by God, he'd have to drive forty miles dead drunk to do it, and there was a good chance he'd kill himself first.

I tell Ross how she cut her own hair to save money. "When she went to class, she wore a madras wraparound skirt that she made and simple navy-blue Keds and an Oxford-cloth shirt. People thought she was independently wealthy."

Ross laughs.

"But money was so tight." I point across the street. "See that experimental ag garden next to the field?"

Ross nods.

"Ann and I used to raid it and help ourselves to fresh produce. We drove Banana Nose crazy."

Ross smiles. "Banana Nose."

"That's what we called the campus maintenance man. A big guy in a stained khaki uniform and a ratty old Stetson. He looked like someone built from spare parts—a giant nose like Jimmy Durante but a little mouth like a slot in a vending machine. And his lips didn't move when he talked, the opposite of bad animation—everything moved *but* his mouth."

Ross laughs.

"One day he caught us picking tomatoes. Chased us across the field in his truck. I mean, the man could've killed us, but we took off running, dodging and weaving and dropping tomatoes until we made it back to this student apartment. Mom was in the living room reading. 'What are you devils doing?' We slapped fresh tomatoes down on the counter."

Ross mugs shock, disapproval. "Mom, that's *stealing*."

"That's what she said!"

We laugh.

"So we didn't do it again. And didn't have to, because her senior year the history department let her teach her own class—an extra hundred dollars a month. I'll never forget the day she brought home two bags of groceries and pulled out dill pickles, potato chips, Coca-Cola . . ."

"You were rich, and you had a little money."

"*So* rich." I tell him what my mother told me:

We lived in the student apartment for two years, from '61 to '63 when I got my BA. I remember sitting in Javelina Stadium when we graduated, and it was the thrill of my life. Daddy told me I was worthless, and I wasn't. I was a star there. They hadn't seen a woman that smart in years. They thought the sun rose and set on me, academically speaking. And that was thrilling to me because they weren't that way toward women then. It was just beginning to turn. No, I wouldn't take anything for the joy and sense of accomplishment. It was one of the most vital experiences of my life. That and raising you all. I was a star.

Ross drives on, past the stadium where Mom graduated.

"That's where Mom used to take me to Javelina Hog football games."

"Javelina Hog?"

"That's what they called their football team."

Ross snickers. "Go Hogs!"

"And they were *good* when I was a girl. We had a great quarterback. I can still remember screaming my head off because the games were so thrilling."

He nods his head, smiling. "I can see that."

He drives back across campus slowly so I can take it all in. I point out where the campus tennis court and pool used to be.

"Ann and I played tennis and swam there all the time. And one day we're lazing around on our towels when this glint caught our eye—a Coke bottle lying there in the grass. That was it, the way we'd get rich! Students left bottles lying all over campus as if they weren't worth two cents to someone who had enough gumption to pick them up and collect the deposit."

Ross raises an eyebrow.

"Yes, you could say this was stealing, but the way we saw it we were also providing a service—free bottle clean-up."

"Situational ethics."

"Precisely. But we had to be careful because Banana Nose was always skulking around, so we lined our bike baskets with towels and filled them with empty bottles when he wasn't looking, and took our loot over to Grayson's store. Bailey Grayson was in sixth grade with us at Flato. Worked every day at his family's store after school. He had a huge crush on Ann. He'd look at her with big puppy eyes while he counted the bottles and gave us our money. He never asked any questions. Pretty soon we were buying Cokes of our own and dropping the bottles into our bicycle baskets. And we could've kept going like that forever . . ."

Ross looks at me. "But?"

"We got greedy."

I explain as Ross drives us toward Ann's old house on Lantana Drive.

"When Mom finished her bachelor's degree—*summa cum laude*—"

"Way to go, Mimaw!"

"—she decided to stay for a master's degree. The history department gave her a small fellowship. But we had to move because the student apartments were for undergraduates only. Her math professor—Ben South, from South Bend—told her about a house for rent in his neighborhood, on Yoakum, a block away from Ann's house on Lantana. A sweet little house with French doors overlooking a big fenced backyard. Ninety dollars a month, so Mom could afford it. She even bought herself a new dachshund—*Hans van Drei*. We moved in when Ann and I finished sixth grade. But we still loved going to campus to play tennis and swim."

"And swipe bottles."

"Oh, yeah. It was summer and there were more bottles than ever. Our bike baskets bulged. So we asked Ben South if we could have some scrap wood from the pile beside his garage, and he said fine. Ann and I built a cover for her Radio Flyer red wagon—a wooden platform that fit right on top. We even designed a trap door so we could quickly slip bottles into the wagon."

"When Banana Nose wasn't looking."

"Right. And we painted it blue."

"Very classy."

"It was. On its maiden voyage, we strolled across campus pulling the wagon and picking up bottles. We had a half-dozen or so when Banana Nose stepped into our path. We stopped. The bottles didn't—*clink clink!* He asked what we had in the wagon. 'Oh, nothing,' we said innocently. 'Mind if I take a look?' He snatched off the cover, revealing the bottles. Ann stared at me with big *oh, shit* brown eyes. I feigned wonder. 'How did those get in there?'"

Ross laughs. "I can just see you two."

"'College property,' Banana Nose mumbled. He pointed to the rack on a vending machine. 'Put them back.' We did, and when the wagon was empty, he slid the cover back on, flipped the trap door up and down contemptuously and snorted, 'Let's go.' He started walking. We followed pulling the wagon. We had no idea where he was taking us—reform school or jail or worse, tell our mothers—but he escorted us to the edge of campus—and his jurisdiction—and told us to keep going. 'And don't come back.'"

Ross laughs. "Busted!"

"Yep. Like you and the Skittles."

He pulls up at a stop sign. We're back at the entrance to campus, beside the iron sculpture of the two javelinas.

"Ann and I crossed Santa Gertrudis right here, the wagon thunking behind us, and cheeked it up University Boulevard back toward our neighborhood. When we'd gone a safe distance, we looked back. Banana Nose was still standing there with his hands on his hips, giving us that slitty-eyed look."

"Did he tell your mother?"

"No, I did. I decided if I told her first, she might cut me some slack. And she laughed her ass off when I told her the story. She'd been such a rascal herself, I think it made her happy to know I was, too. That's when I figured out if I told a good story and made her laugh, she'd forgive just about anything."

Ross gazes innocently up at the sky.

CHAPTER TWENTY-THREE

Yoakum Avenue

"I *know* Yoakum is around here," I tell Ross. "It used to dead-end on this road."

He's driving south on University Boulevard, the same route Ann and I took when Banana Nose kicked us off campus.

"This all looks so different—all these big houses used to be vacant lots, and that mowed grass on the median used to be bushes where Ann and I liked to hide at night with a bucket of water balloons and blast cars that drove by. Until the night we hit a police car."

"Did he catch you?"

"Oh, yeah. Caught us red-handed. Asked us our names. I said, 'Patty Briggs and Ruth Bajza.'"

"Who were they?"

"Friends from Flato."

Ross laughs, scandalized.

"The cop wrote down their names and told us to go home. 'Yep, better go, Patty,' I said to Ann. 'Okay, Ruth!' she said, and we scrammed."

"Jesus, Mom, you were *delinquents*."

"*Puh!*" I say. "Good clean fun. Even Mom thought so."

I remember you and Ann Owens on Yoakum. I have never seen such companions. Absolute bosom buddies. Alter egos. I loved it—how happy you were. And I adored Ann. I think y'all were very good for each other, because you both had so much pizzazz. What one didn't think of, the other one did. You were blissful. Ann was right there on Lantana, and y'all could run back and forth. I never worried about the practical jokes you two pulled. I knew you were good kids. And it was such a safe neighborhood. I knew what was going on, but I gave you the freedom because that's the only way you learn to make decisions.

Ross cocks his head, thoughtful. He stops at the red light on King Avenue, the main east-west drag connecting the King Ranch and Highway 77.

"Okay, we've gone too far."

Ross turns around in an abandoned parking lot reduced to cracked asphalt and weeds and a tall, rusted sign with the bottom half missing, but the name is still there in big block letters outlined in burned-out red lights—SKEE'S.

"Oh, my God, stop!"

Ross slams on the brakes. We lurch forward.

"This was Skee's—the old drive-in! When I was a kid, it was *hopping*. Carhops carrying trays to car windows. Burgers and French fries and Cokes with shaved ice."

"Kingsville's Mel's Diner."

"It was. And it wasn't far from our house, so I *know* we're close."

We take the next left on King and, sure enough, two blocks down, we find Yoakum.

"Turn left here. We lived on this block, the last one before the dead end."

Ross turns left, and he was right—if I were driving I'd kill us, I'm rubbernecking so much. I can't take it in fast enough.

"Go slow," I say.

He drives slowly to the dead end, does a smooth three-point turn, and drives back again, pulling up in front of the house I point out. If he'd asked the address, I couldn't have told him, but I recognize it the minute I see it—1019 Yoakum. A small white frame house with blue trim. A mimosa tree in the front yard. A long skinny driveway leading to the one-car garage with a white metal door.

"I hit a thousand tennis balls against that garage door."

"Your neighbors must've loved that."

"Amazingly, they never complained, but I don't know how Mom got any studying done."

"And the current owner probably thinks we're casing the place."

"I don't care." I sit in the passenger seat, staring at our old house, just soaking it in. Even more than A&I, this takes me back to being a tomboy, especially the summer before seventh grade. That summer was heaven. "Heaven on the half-shell," as Mark Twain once said. Living so close to Ann. Hot days and warm evenings tearing back and forth between our two houses.

I show Ross the shortcut we used to take, a grassy strip between Ben South's brick house and the sagging gray frame house beside it. "That's where the weird sisters lived with their elderly mother."

"Weird sisters as in *Macbeth*?"

"Weird as in they never said one word to us the whole time we lived here. Never introduced themselves or told us their names. So Patty's best buddy from King High, Jimbo Campbell, made up names for them—Injun Squaw, Great White Goddess, and O Ancient One."

Ross chuckles. "Not exactly PC."

"No, but dead on," I said. One sister had long silver braids she unwound every evening out on the porch, brushed out her hair nice and slow, kind of dreamy, and braided it back up. Her sister was brisk, stocky, athletic. Short gray hair. Lived in gym shorts—a PE teacher at A&I. Their mother was older than God, her hair white as cotton."

"Like God's," Ross deadpans.

"O Ancient One would lie in bed all day long with the window open right next to our shortcut. And every time Ann and I shot the gap, Ben South's cat, Lucky, would leap out and hiss and we'd shriek and the poor old lady would moan. All summer long—hiss, shriek, moan."

Both houses look locked up, but the front door of our old house is standing wide open. A big white poodle sniffs at the screen door.

Ross cuts off the engine. "I think you should go in."

"Nah," I say, suddenly shy.

"Oh, come on, Mom. You're *here*."

"I did some remodeling," the owner, Dave, tells us when we go in. He's young, friendly, scruffy, a sweaty bandana hiding most of his curly red hair. Maybe he did remodel, but different décor aside, the space is the same—a living room with French doors overlooking a covered patio and a big fenced backyard. "Y'all look around as much as you like. I'll be outside." He leaves us alone and returns to his yard work.

Ross shoves his hands in his pockets and glances around. "Has it changed?"

"Not all that much, no. The TV was there by the French doors. I remember bouncing in the front door and seeing four British guys in dark suits and strange bowl cuts singing on *The Ed Sullivan Show*."

Ross smiles. "Cool."

"I was lying right there on the rug watching live TV when Jack Ruby shot Lee Harvey Oswald. The shots sounded just like a pop gun. Oswald's mouth popped open and he doubled over in pain. People were screaming. Mom was in the back taking a shower. I ran down the hall screaming, *'Mom! They shot Oswald!'* She couldn't believe that she'd missed it."

"The historian steps out of the room, and history happens."

"Exactly." I turn around. "Our round dining table was right in front of those windows."

"The same table we have now?"

"With the lazy Susan. Mom fell in love with it back in Bethesda, before the divorce. She knew Dad would never give her the money to buy it, but she was such a great manager she saved five dollars a week out of the grocery money he gave her." I look at Ross. "You should know that. It will be yours or Anne's someday."

For a moment, I see Mom and Patty and me at the table eating pinto beans or spaghetti or goulash. My mother, a young graduate student—thirty-four—her hair dark and shiny. My sister, a sophomore in high school—Ross's age—with a bouffant hairdo ratted so high you could see daylight through it. And myself—twelve years old—a gap-toothed tomboy with a bowl cut like the Beatles. "We ate dinner here every night. Mom insisted we spend that time together. And I'd regale them with Ann's and my latest escapade."

"The Great Coke Bottle Heist."

"Bailey and the Bees," I add, laughing.

Ross rocks back and forth patiently in his untied running shoes. "Bailey and the Bees?"

I smile. "Later."

We walk down the hall. "Mom slept and studied in the small bedroom. She finished her master's degree at A&I in 1963, when you could still teach in college with an MA. She applied for teaching positions all over the country. Canada, too. We'd look at the atlas and locate the strange-sounding places we might move to— Chico State, Saskatoon. She also applied to PhD programs, in case no job offers came through. A hundred and forty-four applications all told. She could barely afford the postage to send them."

"That's amazing that you remember the exact number."

"Well, our future depended on them."

We look in the big bedroom. "I had to share this with Patty, who was a *big* disappointment."

Ross laughs, knowing how close I am to my sister now.

"Boy crazy. Mooning or swooning. She'd been like that since we moved to Kingsville, carrying on about boys and clothes and makeup and big hair. Girly shit. She decided to try out for cheerleader, and I heard her practicing cheers in the bedroom, lying here in the dark—*rah rah rah rah!* So I snuck into the room and hid at the foot of the bed and leaped into the air. Scared the hell out of her. She ran screaming and crying to Mom. And swore she'd get even."

"Did she?"

"Oh, yeah, the night Ann and I walked downtown to the Texas Theater and saw Hitchcock's *The Birds*. We walked home at dusk, totally freaked out by the movie. It was dark by the time I got home. The light was off here in the bedroom. Patty was sleeping. I crept slowly across the dark room, terrified that I'd see the guy with his eye eaten out slumped in the corner, so I shut my eyes and groped my way to the edge of the double bed that we shared. I started to pull back the covers when—*brawk!*—Patty squawked like a bird and my taut nerves snapped and the ends of my fingers went numb and I rose into the air and flopped down on the bed, screaming and crying. Patty was shrieking with laughter. Mom came running and I told her what Patty did to me and she said, 'Exactly what you did to her.'

"Patty started laughing again, and I screamed, 'You stupid *girl*!' And Mom escorted me down the hall to the living room and sat me down on the couch. I figured I was in for a lecture but she told me a story: When she was my age, Granddaddy would sneer at her for being a girl, call her 'nature's mistake'—and worse—so one day Mom sneered at her mother for being female. Mamaw sat *her* down on the couch and told her the same thing my mother told me: '*Never* apologize for who you are. Someday you'll be a woman and you're going to be proud.'"

"And she is," Ross says. "And so are you."

I smile. "Absolutely."

We thank Dave and get back in the Mystique and head back down Yoakum. I point out the corner where Ann and I loved to hide on hot summer nights until a car or motorcycle roared by and we'd leap out shouting, "Baroom!"

Ross raises one wooly-worm eyebrow. "Baroom?"

"Varoom with a b."

"And that means . . . ?"

"I have no idea. A cry of freedom. The sheer damn joy of being alive."

"Is that the corner where you stuffed fake dead bodies?"

"Yep. Laid them there on the curb. Roared with laughter when drivers slammed on their brakes."

"You two are lucky you *lived* to be women."

"Really," I laugh. "Turn left here."

Ross drives us down the short, dusty street—Jackson—that Ts at the street in back of Ann Owens' old house, once white, but now a god-awful flesh-colored beige. He pulls up and stops beside the hog wire fence.

"And that's where we hid with Ann's record player and launched Jerome Staggers. It used to be bushes."

"After you two, Kingsville probably banned them."

I laugh. Then I notice something else missing in Ann's old back yard. "The mesquite tree is gone." Fitting, perhaps, since I've given up writing.

But when Ross drives around to the front of Ann's house, the palm tree is still there—a good fifteen feet taller than it was when we covered our bodies with mud and stood side-by-side grinning into the camera. "That's where we slathered ourselves in mud."

"The mud photo!" He stops the car.

"Mom and Harriette were inside. I'll never forget Mom's face—and Harriette's—when we knocked and they opened the door."

Harriette and I were in the house—she was putting lunch on the table—and all of a sudden there was an apparition of mud-covered kids. Talk about germs and filth! But you two were having the best time, laughing and scratching.

No point getting mad at something like that. My mother would've killed me if I'd done it—I irritated the hell out of her—but you two were having a wonderful time. And I decided when I was a kid, I used to say, "When I grow up I won't treat kids that way. I'll give them their freedom." Oh, the mud, the mud. You had plastered it all over your-selves. Ann looking out through that mud, and you, too. There was absolutely no reason to get mad at a child who does that. They need the adventure. You weren't doing anything wrong. You were just wallowing in mud like little hogs. No, it was a riot.

"Ann and I stood there howling with laughter, and Mom and Harriette joined right in. I never laughed harder in my life." I look over at Ross. "Until Mr. San Peppy."

We both burst out laughing.

When our laughter subsides, I roll down my window, smell the warm dusty air, hear the Texas doves calling. I'd forgotten that they sound like owls—*who who who who*!

Oh, I was prepared to be disappointed. I was prepared for this town to have changed. But I wasn't prepared for so much to be exactly the same. And I wasn't prepared for the bliss I feel now reconnecting with place and the person I used to be. Sitting here with my son in the afternoon light, I feel the past and present merge into one—the tomboy I was then and the woman I am now. I feel a wave of emotion—pure elation—break over me. I feel giddy. I feel like shouting, "Baroom!"

I look over at Ross. "Are you having as good a time as I am?"

"I don't think that's possible, Mom," he says, laughing gently, "but I'm having a really good time."

CHAPTER TWENTY-FOUR

The Last Tomboy

"Going to junior high was like being dropped on the Planet Hormone."

Ross laughs knowingly. We're parked on 2nd Street now, alongside the administration offices of the Kingsville Public Schools, formerly Memorial Junior High School. The buildings are the same beige stucco and flat as cow patties, and the mesquite trees are so bent by prevailing winds it looks like they're having a really bad hair day.

"All the girls were like my sister—boy crazy. Obsessed with appearance and similar *shiznit*."

Ross smiles at my use of his word.

"They spent hours ratting their hair."

"Ratting?"

"Back combing so it looks like a rat's nest, then you smooth the top layer and hide the ratting. See also: bouffant."

"Uh-huh," he says.

"Think Jackie Kennedy."

"Ah."

"But Ann and I kept our cap cuts."

"Tomboy badge of honor."

"You got it. All that girl-boy stuff was beneath us. There was no way we were getting sucked in."

Ross snickers.

"But that didn't mean boys didn't love us. Well, Ann."

"Bailey Grayson."

I laugh. "Get out of my head!"

"Is this the part of the movie where you tell me the story of Bailey and the Bees?"

I pull a serious face. "I think it's time." I look at my old junior high school and I'm back in seventh grade with Ann Owens. "Ann played in the band after school, and I played on the tennis team."

"Killer Johnson, right?"

"That's what the coach called me. And, hey, I was good. *Damn* good. So every day after tennis and band practice Ann and I would meet at the breezeway next to the band room—that detached frame building—before we walked home. And we're sitting there one day shooting the shit with Ann Stiles when Bailey Grayson walks out of the band room. He lights up when he sees Ann Owens."

"The boy had it bad."

"I'm telling you. And here's his chance to impress her, prove his male prowess, but how? We could almost see the wheels turning. And just then this Texas-sized bee drones past his pockmarked face and lands on the siding of the band room. Bailey watches it crawl into this little round hole. A second bee drones across the dirt yard and goes into the hole. Then a bee comes out of the hole and takes off nice and lazy to do whatever bees do on warm afternoons in south Texas. Bailey watches it go. We watch Bailey watch it. Then he walks to his bike, dumps his books in his basket, and walks back to the band room. He takes a deep breath and—*bam!*—slaps the band room siding with the flat of his hand. A few pissed-off bees fly out like a shot but he runs away before they can sting him. The three of us laugh, which, apparently, Bailey mistook for approval."

"Uh-oh," Ross says.

"He looks at the bees making this small angry orbit outside their hole and he struts back to them all puffed up like a rooster. Walks right up to the band room and—*wham!*—kicks the wall. *Fifty* bees shoot out like an arrow, straight at him, and he takes off running, flapping his arms. And we're cracking up."

Ross chuckles. "I'm sure you were."

"So Bailey walks back to his bike and pushes it down the sidewalk. We think, *That's it, show's over*, and start to gather our stuff, but Bailey stops and puts down his kickstand and shoots us a proud grin—*the getaway car*."

Ross laughs. "This is going to end badly—"

"*Zzt!*" But I can't help laughing, too. "So Bailey pulls a folder out of his bike basket, rolls it up, and marches back toward the band room. He stops. Eyeballs the bees, which are *swarming* outside their hole. We can't believe what we're seeing. We look at each other—*daylight never shone on so perfect a moron!*—and crack up laughing again. Because he raises the folder over his head and lets out a loud rebel yell and charges, mouth open, but before he even *gets* to the band room the horde of bees goes after him, stinging like crazy, and he runs screaming and yelping straight for his bike but he's so freaked out he runs right past it!"

Ross and I are both laughing hard now, but I manage to finish the story.

"And we're dying, the three of us collapsing on each other, convulsed with laughter watching Bailey disappear down the sidewalk in this big cloud of bees, shrieking and swatting himself in the head."

I'm convulsed with laughter now, too.

Ross laughs with me, at me, at the story? I'm not quite sure.

I take a deep breath. "Anyway, the whole thing rested our tomboy case—if you get caught up in this mating-dance stuff—"

"You get stung."

We laugh again.

Ross drives on down 2nd Street, following Bailey's flight from the bees. We pass the old playground, now a big, empty stretch of short grass.

"Hang on a second."

He knows the drill—and pulls over.

"That was the playground. I was standing right there when I heard that Kennedy had been shot."

Ross winces. "Oh, wow."

"It was after lunch on a Friday, so we were all cutting up, rowdy. Then a teacher came out and made the announcement—*President Kennedy's been shot in Dallas*—and then, a stunned silence. The teacher herded us back to our classrooms. An hour later the principal came on the PA system and told us the president was dead."

Ross slides his hand across the Mystique's steering wheel. "God, Mom."

"I know. It was just . . . time stopped. That's what it felt like. Everyone knows where they were when they heard the news. My sister was standing out on the breezeway at King High. She said her first thought was, *Oh, no, they might cancel the pep rally this afternoon!*"

"Seriously?"

"That's what she told me. Mom was at A&I, coming out of

history class when she heard the news. Aunt Patty and her new husband, Tom, had just moved to Rockport from Corpus. She was grocery shopping when the store owner made the announcement. She said the place went dead quiet, then this guy standing next to her said, 'It's about time they killed that nigger lover!'"

"Jesus."

"This wasn't exactly Kennedy country, but most people were stunned. We were shattered. My mother was born in the year of the Great Crash. She survived the Depression, the rise of Hitler, World War II, Korea, the Cold War, Viet Nam, and Richard Nixon, but she says Kennedy's assassination was the most staggering political event of her life."

"Wow."

"My life, too. That's when I decided to be a historian like her." Ross cuts me a look—*huh?*

"The next day I asked her to drive me to all the newsstands in town so I could buy every newspaper and magazine—*Time, Newsweek, Life.*"

"Do we still have them?"

"I hope so. Somewhere." I try to think where. In the attic, under the rafters, where I've stored so many pieces of my life—from motherhood back to childhood. It's archaeological, really, the layers of life in reverse chronological order.

Like the backseat of the Mystique. It's beginning to look like Ross's bedroom in Tallahassee, but on this, the sixth day of our road trip, I feel an affection for the detritus from all that we've done—brochures from the King Ranch and the National Wildflower Center, the program we bought at the Spurs-Lakers game, the turquoise menu with the black bottom burger, postcards of the Menger lobby and bar for my mother, a bright purple coaster from

Boudro's, a book about the Alamo, two torn IMAX tickets, miscellaneous guidebooks, all well-thumbed by now, Clive Cussler tapes tossed aside as we've finished listening to them, Ross's Frisbee, a pamphlet from the New Orleans Audubon Zoo, and our old atlas, the one we looked at the night we realized we had the same escape fantasy. I pull it from the bottom of the pile. We'll need it tomorrow when we head home.

I gaze again at the playground. "Kennedy's death felt like this odd intersection—the country and I were losing our innocence, coming of age, whether we liked it or not. Ann and I held out as tomboys until spring when Ann got braces and started letting her cap cut grow out. One night in the Texas Theater, she confided that she'd bought a bra—a Littlest Angel."

"Littlest Angel," Ross snickers.

"Grows as you grow."

He laughs.

"I remember asking Ann how it felt. 'Like a big ol' Band-Aid,' she whispered. Then she told me about the upcoming spring dance—and talked me into going. She'd already bought a new dress at Ragland's—ice-blue crepe with tucks down the front. I couldn't tell you what I wore to the dance—something homemade, I'm sure, because Patty and I had to make our own clothes—but I remember Ann's dress. She let me try it on after she bought it. I remember looking in her full-length mirror and thinking, *I almost look pretty*."

"You *are* pretty," Ross says.

"Thank you," I say, and I'm touched that he thinks so, "but I wasn't back then. Mom cut my hair—a real chop job. I was as freckled as she was—'Stood too close to the south end of a chicken heading north,' Mamaw used to tell her when she was a girl. And

I still had this gap between my front teeth. Not that I cared. Until that damn dance. It was your basic junior high nightmare—girls lined up on one side of the cafeteria, boys on the other."

"Been there," Ross says.

"Sagging crepe paper streamers. Beach Boys playing on an old record player. Ann and I lined up with the rest of the girls. Every so often a boy would detach himself from the wall across the room and drift our way. And when the dance was half over, some boy asked Ann to dance. She shot me a guilty look—*sorry!*—but I nudged her—*go on, I'll get my chance*. She started dancing with him, and when the song ended they joined a group of popular kids who'd pulled folding chairs into a circle. Every so often Ann got up and danced."

Ross frowns. "What about you?"

"No one asked."

"No one?"

"Not one boy, all night long."

"Oh, Mom," he says, sympathetic. Then he fake sneezes *loser*.

I laugh. "Oh, yeah, your basic wallflower. And I was *crushed*. But the hardest part was watching Ann and the others dancing and laughing and talking. I had this awful sensation that she was sliding away toward the future and I'd be left behind if I didn't figure out how to fit in. So I went home. Mom asked how it went. I started crying and cried all night long."

"Poor *Mom*."

"It was rough, but you might not be here if that hadn't happened, because by morning I'd decided to be a girl after all."

CHAPTER TWENTY-FIVE

Kleberg Avenue
to 4th Street

I spare Ross most of the details as he drives us downtown, but being female, I discovered, had much to do with the addition and subtraction of hair.

"The hair on my head had to grow. The hair on my legs had to go. That's what Patty told me when she took me under her wing."

"Her own science project."

I laugh. "Teaching me to shave my legs was a snap, but she eyeballed my cap cut like it was something I'd scraped off the road and stuck on my head. I wanted to smack her, but I was too grateful she'd taken an interest. After all, she was a junior at King High and a big shot to boot, going steady with Gary Carley, their football and basketball star. They hung out at Skee's all the time. I remember asking her if he'd kissed her. She laughed like I was some kind of stupid."

"Daylight never shone on so perfect a moron."

"I was so grossed out I said, 'On the *mouth?*' She raised her pinkie. 'No, on the little finger.'"

He chuckles.

"It took forever for my hair to grow out. When it did, Patty showed me how to roll it up on small orange juice cans."

He cracks up.

"I kid you not. Or prickly pink rollers. Then she taught me how to rat, smooth, and flip it. Remind me to show you my seventh-grade school picture—a sixties flip on a freckled-face girl with a big gap-tooth smile. I begged for braces, but Mom said she couldn't afford them and I didn't need them because the gap would close by itself when my wisdom teeth came in. But I couldn't wait, so I hid little round rubber bands under my pillow, and every night when Mom and Patty were asleep I'd wrap one around my front teeth. In a few months, the gap disappeared."

Ross guffaws. "You fixed your own teeth!"

"Hey, I was desperate! And it worked because near the end of the school year, Patty looked almost pleased. 'And guess what?' she said. 'Jimbo's little brother, Dickie, thinks you're cute.'"

Ross angle parks in front of a handsome red-brick two-story building downtown with JB RAGLAND MERCANTILE BUILDING 1804 chiseled over the windows. We get out of the car and go into what is now the King Ranch Saddle Shop.

"Wow," I say, taking in the rich smell of leather from the array of saddles and luggage and purses, all with the Running W brand. "This used to be Ragland's, a super cool clothing store. Mom always said looks were free, so Ann and I haunted this place."

I run my hand across the rough wool of a striped saddle blanket on a long table full of Stetsons. "This is where the old fitting rooms used to be—separate stalls with cloth curtains that never quite closed."

He smiles. "Is that where you bought your first Littlest Angel?"

"As a matter of fact. And it took me so long to figure out how to hook the damn thing, the saleslady yanked open the curtain. I was so painfully modest I cringed in the corner, but did she take the hint? No, she started poking my chest with her bony finger. 'Does it fit? Does it fit?' I like to died."

Ross grins and tries on a white felt cowboy hat.

I pull out the camera and snap a picture before he can stop me.

He scowls at me, at himself in the mirror. "I look like a *dork*."

"You're adorable," I assure him.

"*Puh!*" he says, and puts down the hat.

We stroll the two-block downtown, past Harrel's Pharmacy—now spruced up and expanded—where Ann and I used to drink chocolate malts, then on down Kleberg to the Texas Theater, a real Art Deco gem.

"I didn't know this was Deco," I say, amazed. "It used to be so disgusting. I remember a roach ran across Ann's bare foot in the middle of *Psycho* and she screamed and the whole place went wild." I cup my hands around my eyes and peer in the locked glass front door. The lobby looks recently painted, but from the little I can see of the theater itself, it looks like it still has the same cracked red-leather seats. "Tickets were a quarter. Drinks were a dime. Ann and I always bought Suicides—Coke, Orange, Dr. Pepper, and Sprite."

"Mom," Ross says, "we call it that, too."

I look at him. "Really?"

He mugs—*go figure*.

We cross the street, and I take a picture of the theater.

A woman's voice screeches, "Why did you take that?" She flaps toward us in a tropical house dress, her gray frizzy hair flying. She stops in front of us, out of breath. "Why did you take that picture?"

"I, um, grew up in Kingsville."

"Oh." She leans toward us and whispers, "Then you've seen the vault."

Ross and I exchange glances.

"What vault?" I ask politely.

"Over there! In the loan office! A few doors down from the Texas Theater! It's Mexican silver! Worth a fortune! Nobody knows how much Mexican silver is *worth*!"

Ross shoots me a look—*I think someone shot out her porch light.*

"Tell you what," I say, not without sympathy, given my own mother's dementia. "We'll go have a look."

"I'll show you!" she crows, making a beeline to the loan office.

We follow at a safe distance.

Two women walk out of a store by the Texas Theater. She accosts them. "Hey! Those computers for the public don't work!"

Ross and I tiptoe past while she harangues them.

She wheels around toward us. "Did you see the vault?"

"No," I say, "but we're going—"

She grabs my arm and leads me down the sidewalk, her face close to mine. Her watery eyes are blue like my mother's. I look at Ross over my shoulder. He saunters behind, smiling.

The two young women escape across the street.

"See?" The woman taps on a storefront window. "There it is!"

We look in. Sure enough, against the back wall, there's a big silver door to a bank vault. The beaded border and antique patina of the Mexican silver—if that's what it is—are beautifully polished.

"Wow," Ross says, impressed.

I thank the woman for pointing it out.

"Worth a fortune!" she says.

I glance at my watch—almost six. "Is the public library still close to here?"

"Right around the corner on 4th Street, but those computers don't work!" She sees the two young women getting away. "Hey," she shouts, "about those computers!"

The women duck into Harrel's. She follows them in.

As Ross drives us down 4th Street, I tell him how my sister and Jimbo fanned the flames—well, the spark—of my feelings for Dickie Campbell.

"Did you think he was cute?"

"*Very* cute. Sun-bleached hair and freckles. Super smart. Funny. A cut-up."

"Like you and Ann."

"But a year older—in eighth grade—so I rarely saw him. But we were allowed to leave school at lunch, and the public library was the latest hot spot. High school kids came to study, but cool junior high kids came just to hang out."

"Like Dickie Campbell."

I see the Robert J. Kleberg Public Library ahead on the right, exactly as I remembered—a small red brick building with glass double doors next to a large white stucco addition with a mosaic of the six flags that flew over Texas.

"That's the place, Ross. That's where I test drove my new female self."

Ross glances at me, clearly not sure what I'm talking about.

"I felt like this fragile, newfangled female contraption created by rubber bands, razors, and orange juice cans."

Now he really cuts me a look—*huh?*

"No more gap, no more cap cut, no more hairy legs. My hair was shoulder length, ratted, and flipped. I was even wearing a dress on that fateful day." I can still see the dress that I'd made—a sleeveless apricot kettle-cloth A-line with darts where breasts would, please God, eventually be.

Ross parks across the street in front of a swaybacked house with more appliances out on the porch than I suspect are inside.

And before we go in the library, I tell him the story of My Maiden Voyage as a Flirt. Of all the stories I've told him this trip, this one makes him laugh the hardest. I crack up as I tell it. The Mystique rocks back and forth because we're laughing so hard, even harder than we laughed at Mr. San Peppy.

When our laughter finally dies down, we sit for a moment swiping tears from our eyes. And Ross gives me a look that's worth a parent's price of admission—a mix of admiration and compassion, as if he finally gets that growing up was hard for me, too.

Three small children are peeking in the library's glass double doors, the same doors Ann and I walked in that day.

I roll down my car window and ask the kids, "Is it open?"

"No, ma'am, it's closed," they singsong back.

The lights are off, but I can see the silhouette of a man moving inside. "Hang on, I'll go see." I slip out of the car and walk to the library's entrance and tap on the glass.

The librarian looks up and sees me. He walks over and unlocks the door. "Yes?"

"Hi," I say, a bit sheepish. "I hate to disturb you, but I grew up in Kingsville, and I spent a lot of time here." I let him think I mean reading. "And I'm back with my son." I gesture toward the Mystique.

Ross waves.

"I know you're closed, but I wondered if we could come in and take a quick picture." I hold up my camera.

He smiles. "Sure. I'm Mr. Rodriguez."

I introduce myself and wave Ross out of the car. A puppy on the swaybacked porch sees him and waddles his way. Ross pats the dog and they play for a moment—puppy to puppy—until a woman flies out of the house shouting something in Spanish. She scoops up the puppy and shoots Ross dirty looks.

Ross crosses the street. Shrugs. "I was just playing."

I introduce him to Mr. Rodriguez.

"Come in," the librarian says.

We follow him into the cool dark building.

"Would you like me to turn on the lights?"

"Do you mind?"

"Not at all." He walks to the light switch.

Ross whispers, "Did you tell him the story?"

"Well, *no*."

"I think you should—"

"*Zȝȝt!*"

Fluorescent light fills the room.

I notice new furniture. A more spacious arrangement.

Ross looks around smiling. "This is it, huh?"

"It feels bigger. There were two rows of reading tables right there with an aisle up the middle that led from the front door to the ranges of books in the back."

"Where you saw Dickie Campbell." He waggles his eyebrows.

"Stand over there by that shelf of books."

He makes a deadpan face for the camera.

After I snap the picture, Mr. Rodriguez gives us a quick tour.

"We added a reading room in the back. And a garden. My clientele is mostly Hispanic, and I do all I can to get them to read." He shows us the lush landscaped yard with a redwood gazebo.

"Cool," Ross says. "I'd read there."

I second the motion.

Mr. Rodriguez looks down. Is he blushing? "Please, look around," he says softly. He returns to the circulation desk and starts checking in books.

I stand in the center of the old reading room, remembering how it used to look. Ross walks back to the ranges of novels and flips through one, nonchalantly, close to the spot where Dickie was standing when Ann and I saw him that day.

For a moment, I see Ann and me at thirteen, side by side, as we push open the glass double doors. We check out the scene, scan the kids reading books at the two rows of tables. No one we know. High schoolers. Boring. We're about to walk out when Ann nudges me. I turn around. "What?"

She moves her index finger back and forth under her nose as if she's scratching, a style of pointing we thought was subtle. I look at the back of the room, and there's Dickie Campbell, standing with a couple of buddies between two tall ranges of novels.

Ann whispers, "Go say hello."

I cower. "No!"

"Here's your *chance*."

I just stand there.

"Go *on*." She gives me a gentle shove.

I take an uncertain step.

Ann nudges me up the aisle between the tables of high schoolers, some sleeping, some reading. My nerves feel tighter than they did the night that we saw *The Birds*, but Ann's walking behind me, making sure I don't chicken out. I move closer to the two tall ranges of novels where Dickie is standing, then I panic. "Now what?"

Ann pushes me, whispering, "*Flirt!*"

I balk. But Dickie's only a few feet away, cutting up with his friends, and God almighty, he's cute.

He notices me.

"Oh, hey, Dickie," I say, as if I just saw him.

He smiles but just stands there. His two buddies nudge *him*. He must be as nervous as I am, because he starts making goofy sounds with his mouth—*bleepity bloop, bleepity bloop*.

I toss my flipped hair flirtatiously. "Well, I hope you feel better!"

Dickie laughs.

Success!

Then I feel it—a stab in my gut. Last night's *frijoles* fermenting. Dear God, *no*! I spin around and frantically tell Ann to cover.

She knows the code and coughs nice and loud, but the fart explodes like a pistol.

Dickie recoils as if he's been shot. He and his friends start lurching with laughter—*because the fart doesn't stop*! It roars like a chain saw, a souped-up car engine, a low-flying plane. I turn and run down the aisle, roaring like a crop duster.

High school students lower their books in amazement.

Ann runs a safe distance behind, coughing like crazy.

And the fart doesn't stop until we both burst out the double glass doors and collapse on the grass like two spent balloons.

Ross and I thank Mr. Rodriguez and walk out those same double doors. I point to the place on the grass where Ann and I collapsed laughing. "What else could we do?"

Ross and I laugh all the way to the car.

The woman with the puppy steps out on the porch and eyes Ross suspiciously.

He eases in behind the Mystique's steering wheel. I get in, too. He starts the engine. Cool air blows. "Which way?"

"Head back toward downtown, then turn left on Kleberg."

He pulls away from the curb. "What did the kids at school say?"

"Ken Russell—*the* cutest seventh grader—picked up attendance slips after lunch, and he whispered to me, 'Hey, Claudia! *Plltttt!*'"

We laugh again.

"So I wasn't all that upset when Mom said we were moving to Houston."

News to Ross. "When did you move to Houston?"

"At the end of that summer. I hated to leave Ann, but after the Dickie Campbell fiasco, I needed to make a clean start."

"Yeah," Ross says. "I know the feeling."

I look at him. "Do you?"

"That's one of the reasons I was glad to leave Live Oak and start sixth grade at Maclay. Remember, I'd been Fart Man for Halloween in fifth grade?"

"I remember. I made you a black satin cape with a yellow F on it."

"I got a reputation as Fart Man and I couldn't shake it. I wanted a higher reputation than that."

"Good for you," I say with new admiration. "I had no idea."

"It wasn't the main reason I was happy to move, but it was a small reason, yes."

"God," I say with a laugh, "I'd forgotten Fart Man."

CHAPTER TWENTY-SIX

4th Street to Kleberg Avenue

"Why did you move to Houston?" Ross asks as he drives down 4th Street, backtracking toward Kleberg.

"Because Mom didn't get one of the jobs—or PhD programs— she'd applied for."

Ross is staggered. "Not *one*?"

"Nope, not one. Out of a hundred and forty-four applications."

"That's awful."

"It was. Mom showed me the thick stack of rejection letters. And what so many of them said: 'We want a man for the job.'"

"They actually said that?" Ross says, clearly shocked.

"Sweetie, I saw it with my own eyes. And I was shocked, too. So was Mom."

I can't tell you what it was like. I was told repeatedly, "You women don't belong. Get married. Have kids." I said, "I've been married. I have kids." That was right on the leading edge of the Women's Movement. Thank God for the Women's Movement. I mean, you have to have lived through that. It's like this open bigotry that says that's the way of the world, and if you have a problem with it, it's your problem. What is the matter with these men that they have to treat women this way? God, I was much brighter than most of those men.

"She was so angry she burned them."

"The whole stack of rejections?"

"Every damn one. Set them on fire in our kitchen sink on Yoakum. Watched the edges of the paper blacken and curl. Washed the ashes down the sink."

"Then what did she do?"

"There wasn't a whole lot she *could* do. Apply to teach at King High, but she said she'd rather be dead. So she consoled herself with her work. Holed up in her bedroom and finished her master's degree. She wrote a bang-up thesis that summer about a Brit named Schuster and the British presence in the Middle East. She even learned Persian. I loved watching her write it, the way the words flowed right to left. British History was her bliss—especially the nineteenth century. She loved Kipling, and after she burned the rejection letters, she took to reciting his *Barrack-Room Ballads*. One verse is still burned in my brain:

When you're wounded and left on Afghanistan's plains,
And the women come out to cut up what remains,
Just roll to your rifle and blow out your brains,
An' go to your Gawd like a soldier.

"Jesus," Ross says.

"I think she was a little depressed."

"I guess so."

"Then her major professor at A&I, Irving Smith, went to bat for her. Browbeat the history department at Rice to take her into their PhD program. They agreed, on one condition—she had to study Austrian history. Mom *hated* Germanic culture."

"Nazis. I hate those guys," Ross says, quoting my favorite Indiana Jones line.

"But that was the deal. Take it or leave it. So one night at dinner on Yoakum, she announced we'd be moving. Patty dissolved. Her life in Kingsville was perfect. She loved Gary. Gary loved her. She was absolutely shattered. But Mom had no choice."

"And she decided that Austrian history was better than nothing."

I nod. "So was getting out of south Texas, because at the end of the summer, the Mamaw and Granddaddy shit hit the fan."

Dad called one evening and said, "Peggy, you have to come over. Your mother is going to kill me. You're the only one who can control her. You've gotta come and take care of her." And I thought, *Oh, whee!* I remember telling y'all that Granddaddy and Mamaw were off again, and I had to go over and deal with it. So I drove to Corpus and had to spend from about eight in the evening until one o'clock in the morning. When I got there, Mother was out in the kitchen stabbing the washing machine with a butcher knife saying, "I'm going to kill you. I'm going to cut your goddamn heart out!" Daddy was standing stock still on the sun porch. I've never seen him so terrified.

I told Mother to give me the knife. When she looked at me her eyes softened, and she looked at me like a petulant little girl who knew she'd been bad, but when she looked at him her eyes were on fire again. All the rage came back. She was absolutely murderous. She was going to kill Daddy. Oh, we knew why! So did he. That's what he was scared of. Because he had been beating on her, and he had driven her to the point where she couldn't stand it any longer. Really, how much of that can you take? She was murderous, and I don't blame her.

An ambulance took her to Spohn Hospital. They tested her, and she had no insulation left on her nerve ends. She was shorting out. I'm surprised she didn't die. Up in her hospital room she started having god-awful hallucinations, screaming because she thought her teeth were falling out. She was on a bad trip because she'd been poisoned by drugs.

The next day they put her in a straitjacket. You have to wonder why they did that when they could have sedated her. It was so humiliating. She was standing in a corner of a padded room like a little child looking up at me. I went up and hugged her. I think that helped her turn a corner. It calmed her down. It helped her subdue her rage. I hugged her, and her body went from stiff to limp. She didn't think that anyone cared.

Ross drives in silence down Kleberg.

"Mom didn't tell us how bad it was—how bad it had been—until she got back the next day. She said we were old enough to know. We sat on the foot of her bed, and as she told us what happened, I pictured her driving to Corpus through night as black as the dirt all around, past the eerie white smoke of the Celanese plant, gripping the steering wheel, her jaw tight with worry, hoping and praying the car wouldn't break down. Wondering what she'd find when she got there. Wishing maybe that Mamaw *would* kill him. I pictured her pulling into their driveway, her headlights raking the front bedroom where Patty and I slept when we first got to Texas. Wondering why she ever came back. Cutting off the engine and sitting there a minute, alone in the dark. Getting out of the car. Walking up the steps and opening the front door."

"How long was Mamaw in a straitjacket?"

"I don't know. Until she calmed down. They put her on mild tranquilizers. That's what she was taking when we moved to Houston that August. Mamaw was more upset about us going than Patty. When Mom told her we were leaving, she cried and begged, 'Take me with you.'"

She said, "You can't leave me." She wanted to go with us because he was being mean to her again. And she was horribly dependent on me, so what could I do? She was my mother.

Ross looks over at me. "Did you take her to Houston?"

"Mom agreed, on one condition—Mamaw couldn't tell Granddaddy where we were going. She couldn't tell him *that* she was going. She had to pack on the sly and sneak out. Mom drove over to Corpus, and they waited until Granddaddy left the house, then they threw Mamaw's things in the Plymouth. Mom said her palms were sweating, she was so scared."

It was like Jews fleeing Hitler. If he'd caught me helping
Mother escape, he'd've killed us for sure.

"So, yes," I tell Ross, "we took her to Houston."

CHAPTER TWENTY-SEVEN

Kleberg Avenue

"Were you happy in Houston?" Ross asks, pulling over and parking, at my request, across from a small, run-down frame house on Kleberg.

"I was, which is kind of amazing. Because there were times when I felt like Anne Frank. I didn't know if Granddaddy would find us or not, but no one ever talked about that. Mom holed up in her room reading Austrian history. Mamaw lay in her bedroom belching and moaning, don't ask me why. And Patty spent half her time crying in the back room we shared and the other half listening to music on this dinky transistor radio Mamaw gave her. I'd slip outside in the evening, partly to get away from the gloom and partly because I loved the blue hour."

"The blue hour?"

"Just before it gets dark, and everything is saturated in blue."

"Ah."

"So I'd sit in the backyard and sway back and forth on this rope swing. I enjoyed being alone—that was a real discovery for me. I think I needed time by myself to grow up, mature. I missed

Kingsville, too, especially Ann, but I started to like who I was becoming."

Ross doesn't say anything. He seems deep in thought, staring into the distance. At his own life? His future? At who he's becoming?

"And I liked my new school—John J. Pershing Junior High. I remember sitting on a stool in the new science lab, giving an oral report about bats."

Ross smiles. "Free tailed?"

"No, vampire. And the report was silk off a spool, to quote Thornton Wilder. I felt so *poised*, a real first. It's funny. I don't remember the words, but I remember the feeling—grown up, I guess you could say."

"Nice," Ross says.

The sun starts to dip behind the small frame house across the street, turning the top of the mesquite tree in the front yard a deep gold.

"So, yes, I was happy. But nobody else was. I do have one memory of Mamaw when she seemed happy. We were in the kitchen, and I asked her to teach me the Highland Fling. She stood up and pointed her toe and started dancing as she sang 'Scotland the Brave,' incredibly light on her feet, her dark wavy hair bouncing. It was this wonderful moment. Most of the time she just lay in bed. She never went anywhere. Neither did Patty, except to school, which she hated, or to the Houston zoo a few times so I could see the raccoons."

Ross laughs. "Why raccoons?"

"I'd just read *Rascal*. I plagued Mom for my own pet raccoon, but she said no way, we couldn't afford one, so I made Patty take me to see them. She didn't mind."

"Any port in a storm."

"Right. Even her little sister. I remember giving the raccoons sugar cubes."

"Why?"

"Ever watch a raccoon try to wash one?" I imitate a bewildered raccoon moving its paws through the water."

"Mom, you're going to hell."

"Hey, I made it up to them."

"How?"

"I shined pennies with an eraser. Raccoons love shiny objects."

He frowns. "I know. That's how they trap them in north Florida. The raccoon reaches into the trap and grabs the shiny object, but its fist is too big to pull out, and it won't let go. The hunters kill it and use the skin to train their dogs to hunt other raccoons."

I grimace. "And you say *I'm* going to hell."

We sit there a moment, listening to the Texas doves hooting.

"My mother thought Corpus was hell, until she got to Houston. She hated Rice, and Patty hated her, and Mamaw hated being without her possessions."

See, that was her, "Boo hoo, I can't live there with him. You have to take me with you." Well, then I did, and she no sooner got up there and she started missing her home and blaming me for dragging her off. This went on for six weeks. Finally, she and I had really ugly words in the kitchen one night. She was in her nightgown. I was cooking. She started whining and griping, "I miss your father. I miss my house and my car and my dishes."

"What kind of car?"

"A yellow DeSoto."

She loved that car, so she started in about how she missed it. Oh, whine and gripe and gripe and whine. I mean, just as nutty as a goddamn fruitcake. So I screamed, "You want to go back to that?" I let her have it verbally right between the eyes. I told her that she'd pull her load and stop acting like an asshole. I had to read three hundred pages a day, and I had two kids, and all she did was think about herself. I still feel bad because I turned on her that night, but I was at the end of my rope. And Patty was so depressed. And no one loved me, either. So we had an exchange of words, and she called Daddy.

"She called him?"

"She did."

"So he knew where you were."

"Mamaw told him. Mom was furious, I mean *livid*. She didn't know if we'd live through the night. None of us did. But we got up the next morning. Patty and I went off to school. And when we got home, Mamaw was gone."

Dad's brother, Kenneth, came up and got her. And she sort of strutted out, saying, "I'm going home." I told her, "If you go back, don't come to me with your troubles again." Then she said, "Well, I just have to go home. I have to have my things."

"Her shiny objects," Ross says. "She couldn't let go."

"No, she couldn't," I say, deeply moved by his wisdom. "But Mom could."

I remember sitting at my desk in my bedroom in Houston, wondering what it would be like to have five hundred dollars. I was running out of money. I was sitting at my desk, and I thought, I hate Austrian history. I hate Rice. I hate the program—a bunch of piss ants. Who needs it? Mamaw was gone. And I was worried sick about Patty. I thought about it all day. I was thirty-five. There was plenty of time to get my PhD, but Patty was only in high school this once. That's when I made my decision. Because I knew how unhappy she was. And I could not do that to her. If it made her that unhappy, it wasn't worth it. I figured I could go back to Kingsville and let her finish high school. I wanted to do that for her. That's how much I loved her. If I had liked it in Houston, I still would have left because she was so unhappy. I remember her smiling through her tears when I told her we were moving back. It was the best thing I could have done for her. No, I couldn't be happy if my children weren't happy. I would do anything to help y'all be happy. So we moved back. We rented that little house on Kleberg. Remember we painted the whole inside of the house? The carpet smelled so bad. It smelled like the Texas Theater. "The Chicken House"—that's what we called it. But I loved being back in Kingsville. Patty was thrilled to death to get back. You both were. We were so damned poor, but we were happy.

Ross looks across the street. "So that's the Chicken House there?"

"That's it. And that's what we called it, because the small gabled front porch looks like a beak."

"Yeah, kinda," he says.

"We lived there the rest of the school year. Gary came over every night to do homework with Patty. She was in heaven. And Ann and I got to hang out again. She said I was more sophisticated, and maybe I was. Boys actually asked me to dance."

Ross chuckles. "Amazing."

"Nicky Harrel asked me to go steady."

Ross raises one eyebrow. "Any relation to Harrel Drugs?"

"He's the pharmacist now."

"Why didn't you stop in to see him?"

"This was back in eighth grade. Thirty-four years ago. I doubt he'd remember." I smooth the nap of my gray velour armrest. "And Nicky dumped me."

"Oh, sorry," Ross says.

"It's okay," I say, droll. "I think I'm over it now."

"Why'd he dump you?"

I laugh just thinking about it.

"Don't tell me—more pinto beans."

"No, this time it was my big fat mouth. We were at a party. The rumor was flying that Nicky was going to kiss me. It took him all evening to build up the courage, but he finally did." A French kiss, I remember, but I'm not telling Ross. Such a surprising, sweet, electric sensation . . .

"Hello, Mom?" He's staring at me.

"Right," I say. "So he kissed me. And I said, 'Oh, Nicky, am I the first girl you ever kissed?'"

Ross gapes. "Tell me you didn't say that."

"I did. I was trying to be romantic, but I guess he thought I thought he couldn't kiss."

"I guess *so*."

"But he could." *Boy, could he.* "Anyway, he dumped me the next day."

Ross cracks ups. "Oh, Nicky, am I the first girl—"

"Hey, if I hadn't said that, you might not be here."

A big dog—Rottweiler? Pit bull?—appears at the Chicken House's chain-link fence gate and starts barking. The owner—renter?—steps out on the front porch and gives us the hairy eyeball, as Ann and I used to say.

Ross sees him, too. "Do you want me to ask him if you can go in?"

"Nah," I say. "It's getting late. And we need to find a motel."

But first, one last stop—519 College Place.

CHAPTER TWENTY-EIGHT

College Place

Ross parks in front of the well-tended, yellow-brick ranch house I point out on College Place.

"This was our last home in Kingsville, and the first house we owned."

"How did you afford that?"

"Mom taught high school Patty's senior year."

"I thought she'd rather be dead."

"Oh, she *hated* it, but she did it for Patty—and applied like crazy to PhD programs. She was making more money than she'd made in her life, so she bought this house." I gaze at the two big trees in front. "The yard was bare when we bought it. A new subdivision. Stark. Soulless. I never liked it—I was too far from Ann—but Mom loved it. No more rentals. And each of us finally had our own bedroom." I shoot Ross a guilty glance. "I have a confession."

"What?"

"My room looked like yours."

"Like landfill?" A trace of bitterness wafts my way.

"Actually, worse."

He laughs, vindicated.

I look back at the house. "It's funny."

"What?"

"We lived in five houses in five years—from the yellow brick student apartment to this yellow brick burger. We lived here most recently, but it's the place I remember the least. Except for three moments I'll never forget."

I tell Ross about them:

The first—a summer day, 1965.

"We'd only been in the house a few weeks. Mom had built her ritual bookcase—floor to ceiling this time—on the wall of the living room across from the couch where she was reading that day. Patty was off somewhere with Gary. Ann Owens was busy. I was lolling around on the living room carpet, fourteen years old and bored—*bored out of my gourd*, as we used to say. I gazed up at the bookcase and plucked *The Canterbury Tales* from the shelf, glancing at the blurb on the back. 'Oh, terrific,' I said. 'A bunch of pilgrims going to church.' Mom lowered her book and suggested that I read 'The Miller's Tale.' I flipped the pages and started to read with utter indifference—*Some time ago there was a rich codger, who lived in Oxford and took in a lodger*—but as the bawdy tale began to unfold, I started lurching with laughter, amazed that *literature* could be so alive, so damn *funny*. Especially when I came to the passage—*This Nicholas at once let fly a fart, as loud as if it were a thunder-clap. Absalon was near blinded by the blast*."

"Like Dickie Campbell."

We laugh.

"I couldn't believe it—*Chaucer wrote about farts!* I felt a moment of healing, balm for my public humiliation, followed by a wave of self-forgiveness, permission to accept myself, farts and all. And in that moment, I realized that stories connect, stories heal, stories leap centuries and change people's lives, because 'The Miller's Tale' had just changed mine. And I decided that I wouldn't study history like my mother. I would study literature."

"And you did," Ross says.

"Remarkable, huh? We really are the sum total of our decisions."

He cocks his head, thoughtful. "Who said that?"

"I'm not sure," I say. "Aristotle?"

The second—the week before Memorial Day, 1966.

"We'd lived here almost a year. I was finishing junior high, and Patty was finishing high school. Mom was still waiting to hear if any PhD program would take her. Mamaw had cancer. She'd beaten breast cancer twice in the forties, but it was terminal now. The cancer had spread all over her body. She'd just broken her hip. She had double pneumonia. Granddaddy called to tell Mom he could not let Mamaw suffer."

He was going to kill her—put her down—as a favor. Mother didn't want him to do it. She said, "You let me die the way I'm supposed to." He'd almost killed her so many times because he was angry, but now I was afraid he'd kill her because he believed she'd be better off.

"Mom told Patty and me we'd have to fend for ourselves because she had to go to Corpus again. We didn't ask any questions. She drove to their house to get Mamaw and check her into Spohn Hospital. Granddaddy met her at the door, but he didn't resist."

I'll never forget the way that he looked. He was sixty-four. It was early in the morning. He was always a little, thin man. He had his pants on and he was barefoot, trying to sober up. He couldn't deal with her being sick. He couldn't cook. His blond hair was a mess, and he was wearing his sleeveless undershirt.

"Wifebeater," Ross says, then winces. "I guess it's time to dump that expression."

The third—the week after Memorial Day, 1966.

"The phone rang in the kitchen. Mom answered. It was Aunt Patty. Granddaddy was dead. He'd killed himself."

My first thought was, *Thank God. For him.* He was so unhappy—he made us all so unhappy—the hell he created, and we got caught in the storm because we cared about Mother.

"He committed suicide?" Ross asks, almost a whisper.

"Yes."

"Why?"

"Mom said he hit rock bottom." I tell him what she said:

He thought Mother was dying. The doctor thought she'd die that weekend, so he called Dad and told him, "You'd better come. Your wife's dying. She won't live until tomorrow." And he couldn't live without her. Oh, the irony. He loved her and couldn't live without her. Absolutely adored her. That's the saddest thing—Mother and Daddy adored each other. Happiness was right there at hand for them, but they couldn't see it. He adored her, but he beat the hell out of her to prove he was more powerful. But I think that day, Memorial Day, he took a hard look at his life. His wife was dying. His children were scared of him. And he was broke. The doctor told him Mother's medical bills would be about $15,000. He had an insurance policy that paid single indemnity for suicide. So maybe it was a little bit noble. His insurance paid her medical bills.

Ross looks over at me. "Do you think what he did was noble?"

"Oh, sweetheart, who knows? Yes and no. His death paid Mamaw's medical bills, but he blamed Mom in his suicide note. If he'd taken responsibility for his own life—and death—it would've been noble."

"Do you know what he said in the note?"

"'Every trouble I've had is because of you.' Something like that. Aunt Patty told Mom the gist, but she wouldn't show her the note. She destroyed it. So we'll never know."

There's a silence, and I sense Ross summoning the courage to ask the next question. "How did he do it?"

I look at his slender face in the waning light. How much should I tell him? I remember clearly what my mother told me, but there are some things a sixteen-year-old does not need to know.

He was dead for three days before anyone found him. The mailman smelled him. It was summer. Hot. Humid. The air conditioner had broken. The coroner said there were blowflies all over him. In his eyes. His eyes were open. The flies laid eggs in his eyes. As the coroner pieced it together,

Daddy stood at his desk in the sunroom, his back to the backyard. He stood with a .22 pistol and shot himself in the forehead. But there were two holes, two shots. The coroner said the first one didn't take. So Daddy shot himself again. Then he turned and walked to their bedroom. You could tell by the trail of blood. Ten or fifteen feet to the adjacent room, got to the bed, turned as if he was going to lie down, then he dropped to the floor. He was holding the gun in his hand. How like him to do that! He always wanted to die in a blaze of glory. And take us with him. But what chance did he have? His father beat him with a horsewhip. And his mother would corner him behind the bathtub when he was little and beat him until he was exhausted. A few days after they found him, I had to go into that house, to their bedroom, to get some stuff for Mother, and I saw the outline there on the floor where he had melted. His body fluids had melted into the floor as he decomposed. I could see where his hand lay turned out to the side. You can't tell me that house isn't haunted. I never went back after I saw that stain on the floor. He melted into the floor.

I look at Ross, backlit by the sinking sun, and I say, "He shot himself. Twice. In the forehead."

CHAPTER TWENTY-NINE

Highway 77

Ross stops at the red light at King Avenue. To our left, toward the King Ranch, the setting sun cracks like an egg on the hardpan horizon.

The light turns green. Ross turns right, and we head east toward Highway 77, the same direction my mother drove us after Aunt Patty called and told her Granddaddy was dead.

"That's my strangest memory—that drive back to Corpus in the metallic-green Rambler that Mom bought with her teaching money. North on Highway 77, past the Celanese plant to the Chapman Ranch Road. I sat in the back seat. Patty rode shotgun. She turned on the radio. News. 'A prominent businessman died last Monday when he took his own life.' I sat there, struck by the 'prominent businessman' part. We'd lived on so little so long, I didn't know there *was* prominence anywhere in the family. *A prominent businessman died last Monday when he took his own life*. The news played it twice, on the hour and the half hour. I remember how strange it felt sitting in the back seat hearing some stranger talk about the very event that was taking us back to Corpus. Hearing him talk about our own family, our flesh and blood dying, and knowing the whole world was hearing it, too."

"That must've been hard."

"It was."

"What about Mamaw?"

"Mom went to see her at Spohn Hospital." I tell him what she told me:

I remember going into the hospital after Dad died. Her long-time doctor, Dr. Collier, went in with us. He held her hand and he said he had some bad news. "Your husband is dead." She started crying. I thought, *Oh, Christ*, then I realized they were tears of relief. She said, "Do you mean I don't have to be afraid of him anymore?" And Collier said, "No, you don't have to be afraid ever again." And tough old Scot that she was, she lived another six months. Six months of happiness. She stayed in the hospital. She felt safe there—and taken care of, the way she'd always wanted. It was heaven for her at the end, even though she was dying.

Ross looks at me, clearly moved. "That's beautiful, Mom."

"It is, isn't it? A miracle, really—Mamaw died happy."

We savor this in silence a moment.

"I don't remember anything else until Granddaddy's funeral. The cemetery was out Ocean Drive, on the way to the UCC pool where Mom walked on her hands down the diving board in her white bathing suit. Overlooking the bay where Granddaddy took us all fishing. It was windy. I must've been looking down most of the service because I remember the skimpy crabgrass and little red stinging ants. Piss ants, we called them. I hated the way they humped up when they stung you. It's crazy what you remember. I mean, my grandfather's funeral and I can't remember what I was feeling. Relief, I guess, like everyone else, especially Mom."

When they lowered the casket, I thought, *Frankenstein's dead. We could have a life. The hell was over.* I've never read a book or seen a movie that was worse—the terror. It's Alfred Hitchcock, but this was a real horror story. I can't tell you the nightmare of having a father like that. It was a torment. And his living was a torment for him. I thought, *Thank God it's over.* Living with a raving—a crazed alcoholic. No, hell doesn't frighten me anymore. I learned courage in the face of real fear. And I'm grateful for what I have. I'm me, and I made what I am. I built a life for myself.

Ross sits, deep in thought, then, "That's so sad," he says. "That your own family would be glad that you're gone."

"Yes," I say softly. "If memory—the way we're remembered— is our afterlife—"

"He's in hell?"

"I don't know. Maybe. I wouldn't presume." I tell Ross my vision of hell—a dark screening room where we have to watch a replay of our life. "Every moment we missed—our children, the sunsets—because we were preoccupied. Every time we were shits to the people we loved. Every lousy choice that we made."

Ross nods. "And the effect it had on others."

As we pass downtown—Ragland's, Harrel's Pharmacy, the Texas Theater—I tell Ross the end of our Texas story. "After a whole lot of browbeating by Mom's professors and colleagues at A&I, Oklahoma University agreed to accept her into their PhD program in British history. At the end of the summer of 1966, we moved to Norman, Oklahoma. I was about to be a sophomore, like you."

"How did you feel about leaving Kingsville?"

"The way I feel now. I love being here, but I'm ready to go."

"On to the next great adventure," Ross says, quoting my father.

"Even Patty was ready. Gary was leaving for college. He got a football scholarship at—get this—*Rice*."

Ross laughs.

"That's what I love about family history—the irony. Before we left Texas, Mom drove back to Corpus to say goodbye to Mamaw, who knew it was the last time she'd see Mom, but she was happy for her, the life she was building. 'I just wish you were married, then I'd know you were safe,' she told Mom. They looked at each other and had a good laugh."

"Nice," Ross says, smiling. "And what about you and Ann?"

"She was sad we were leaving, but we promised we'd stay in touch."

"Good job, Mom. And Mimaw got her PhD."

"In record time—three years."

I was so appreciated by my professors. They appreciated me as a student, and they also thought I had valuable potential as a teacher. And I taught history and economics for twenty years.

Ross smiles. "Now that's what I call a happy ending."

"Indeed." So happy it makes my eyes well.

"And speaking of endings . . ." He shoots me a sly smile and slides in the last Clive Cussler tape. As we drive the rest of the way across Kingsville, we listen to the thrilling conclusion—a show-down between Dirk Pitt and his mortal enemy, Arthur Dorset.

"Pitt touched his finger against the trigger of the assault rifle. 'Get moving, Arthur, or I'll shoot off your ears.'"

"'Go ahead, you yellow bastard.'"

And Dirk Pitt does it. "The gun spat with a loud pop and a slice of Dorset's left ear sprayed the carpet."

Pitt prevails, killing Dorset. And *Shock Wave* mercifully comes to an end.

I pop out the tape. "Well, Ross, I have to be honest. That is the *worst* writing I've ever heard."

Ross beams. "I know. That's why you needed to hear it."

I blink. "You had an *agenda?*"

He slides on his Oakleys. Cool. The essence of cool. "I wanted to raise your self-esteem as a writer."

We pass fast-food places clustered close to the highway. Skee's may have bit the dust years ago, but this strip is thriving. Ross slows down behind a battered red pickup that's poking along. "Get moving, Arthur, or I'll shoot off your ears," he says, but he doesn't tailgate.

In between the signs for the usual fare—McDonald's, Burger King, Taco Bell—I see a sign advertising El Jardin.

"Great honk!" I shout—one of my mother's favorite expressions. "It *is* still here!"

Ross looks at the sign. "Let's definitely go there for dinner."

"You're on. After we find a motel."

He stops at the last traffic light. Highway 77. The route Mom and Patty and I took when we drove north to Norman and left

Texas for good. The route Ross and I will take tomorrow when we head back to Interstate 10.

I scan the motels north and south. "How about a Best Western?"

"Best Western," Ross chuckles. "Sure," he says. "It has a nice ring."

The traffic light changes.

He crosses the highway and pulls in under the motel's overhang. "Jesus, I need a shower."

He does.

"A shower, then it's El Jardin, baby."

El Jardin. The Garden. Paradise.

"Yes," I say, "it is."

Wednesday, April 15, 1998

Trip budget: **$128.84**

Best Western: −$53.11 (Visa)

Balance remaining: **$75.73**

CHAPTER THIRTY

Best Western

"What's it like seeing Kingsville again?" The henna-haired woman at the front desk leans on the counter, eager to know.

"Wonderful," I tell her. "Strange," I add, searching for the right word. "A little surreal. Like seeing a movie set of my childhood."

"Wow," she says, and I can tell she means it. "I've been here all my life." She hands me a heavy brass key. "Enjoy your last night. Continental breakfast here in the morning. Coffee, juice, donuts, and speckled bananas."

I smile at this and return to the car where Ross waits, engine running.

"Room 238, overlooking the pool. Fifty-three bucks a night." I pull out my journal and post what I spent.

"How much do we have to get home?"

"According to my calculations . . . seventy-five buckaroos, minus what we spend on dinner. But that's enough to take us to Ann Tilton's tomorrow and Tallahassee the next day. We should come in right on budget."

We laugh and high five.

Ross pulls around the corner and parks in front of the stairs leading up to our room.

I slide my journal back in my purse. "Hey, thanks for driving today."

"Thanks for bringing me, Mom." He cuts off the engine. "It's been one of the coolest trips ever."

"Has it?" I say.

"Spending so much time with you."

I was prepared for him to mention the Spurs-Lakers game or the Alamo, maybe, but not time with me. I'm so touched and surprised, all I can manage is, "Ah."

"And thanks for giving me a childhood that wasn't traumatic."

I smile. "Well, damn it, I *tried*."

Our room's a nice size—two queen-sized beds with green and burgundy jacquard-print bedspreads. A framed print of flamingos. Fitting—tomorrow morning we head back to Florida.

"Neither gross nor grand," Ross says, looking around. Then, a bit wistful, "I guess the adventure is over." He drops his duffel on the floor, swipes the remote off the nightstand, and turns on the TV as he falls on his bed.

I walk to the window. The color of the sky is lovely—pale yellow. Lemon sky. Drawing the drapes, I feel drawn back again, an inexplicable longing to take a last look at Kingsville before the light fades completely. "Hey, mind if I do one more lap around town?"

"You do that, Mom," Ross says, channel surfing. "I'll take a shower. When you get back, we'll hit El Jardin."

When I said seeing Kingsville again was like seeing a movie set of my childhood, I was not being clever. It's a feeling I've had all day, but I feel it more now as I move through the streets in this small black Mystique. A sense that this place isn't quite real or rooted, that it's hovering between past and present—memory's magic carpet ride. A rising awareness that time is a spiral, that I've come back to this town but I'm somewhere above it, looking down like an aerial shot as I glide over the geography of my childhood— the Texas Theater, Ragland's, Harrel's Pharmacy, the library, Memorial Junior High, the Chicken House, the barroom corner on Yoakum, the back of Ann's house where we climbed the mesquite tree, the palm tree out front where we took the mud picture, Texas A&I's campus.

The elation I felt earlier slowly deepens, like the lemon light going golden. I feel a tenderness toward this town, that time, the tomboy I used to be. Toward my mother and the freedom she gave me. Her astonishing courage.

I park in front of our old student apartment and gaze at the field of grass and mesquite where Ann and I used to run like wild horses. The Wild Horse Desert.

I remember how displaced I felt the day we arrived, how I *hated* the last line of *The Yearling*: "Somewhere beyond the sink-hole, past the magnolia, under the live oak, a boy and a yearling ran side by side, and were gone forever." I refused to believe it was true. And sitting here now thirty-seven years later, I know that it isn't. With all due respect to Marjorie Rawlings, we don't lose important parts of ourselves, we just lose touch with them. Psychic road kill. Somewhere beyond the student apartment, past the mesquite, under the pin oak, two tomboys run side by side, as long as memory lasts.

I drive back across campus, taking it in one last time—the Administration Building, the two red-tiled ramps flanking the Theater

Building, the old biology building beyond. I see a middle-aged man—a professor, perhaps—walking out of the new Earth Sciences building. I park by the sign—JOIN US HERE FOR THE FUTURE—and go in.

There's a glass-front display case in the foyer—the skeleton of an eight-foot alligator. Florida again. Once, on Interstate 10, I saw a gator this size on the side of the highway, but its hide was so black and bumpy I thought it was a blow-out—until it opened its mouth and hissed at the traffic.

I turn to leave and notice another glass-front display—THE HUMAN FETUS DEVELOPMENTAL STAGES. Two rows of specimen jars against a cobalt-blue background. Human fetuses in formaldehyde. In the first jar, a fetus the size of a tadpole, and in the last jar, a pair of near-full-term Siamese twins—the same babies I gaped at when I was a girl.

I'm floored. *Staggered.* Of all the details of my childhood, this is the last one I expected to see. But here they are, almost forty years later, the baby closest to me still resting its head on the bowed head of its twin. Their skin looks papery, fragile, like phyllo. Otherwise, they haven't changed.

But I have. When I look at them, I no longer think of insepa-rable buddies or freak shows. I think of their mother, how heart-broken she must have felt when she lost her babies. I think of the day Ross was born, his head pink and round as a grapefruit, and my primal in-the-blood yearning to hold him. How I hounded the nurses in between feedings—*I want my baby! Bring me my baby!*

I look at the Siamese twins, and I think of Mamaw and Grand-daddy. I could never understand why they destroyed one another, but I was looking at it here all the time. They couldn't let go.

"They couldn't let go, and because they couldn't, they destroyed each other," my mother told me. She insisted they adored one another. Maybe they did, but it wasn't love. Love is something else, something closer to freedom. *Free*, from the Old English *freon*—to love. If you truly love, you let the one you love become who they are. You let go. *Freon—to set at liberty, loose one's hold of*. If you love, you let go, and if you let go, love stays.

I look at the baby closest to me, its tiny right hand curled in a fist that rests on its knee, as if it's making an important decision. A resolution. I think of Ross's resolve to leave home a year early. Do I love him enough to let go? The answer comes quickly—*yes*—leaving me with a mixture of lightness and loss.

I drive back to the Best Western, park the Mystique, and walk slowly up the stairs to our room. The light is brassy, the air soft and balmy. A child splashes out in the pool.

I unlock our door and go in. Ross is right where I left him, sprawled on the bed, his feet hanging over the side, but he isn't watching TV. He's writing on a Best Western note pad.

He leaps up, laughing. "I'll go take that shower!" He rifles his duffel.

I glance at the notes that he's scrawled:

Players line up in the center of the field. You play either as thrower or first man in the stack.

I look at him. "What's all this?"

"Instructions," he says, rummaging through his dirty clothes. "About Ultimate. You know how I haven't felt challenged in school?"

I drop my purse on my bed. "It's boring as piss."

"And it's my fault! So next year I'm loading my schedule with six AP courses and one honors class. Senior year, I'll do dual enrollment."

My heart goes *squish squish*. "I thought you wanted to graduate early."

"I've figured out it's better to stay for my senior year. Because I want to start an Ultimate team at Maclay. Teach others to play. Spread the spirit." He pulls out his Dopp kit and grins at me—*ta da!*

"Can you handle six AP classes?" I ask, sounding like some prim asshole, because what I feel coming is a tsunami of joy and I don't want to drown the boy in it.

"*Mom!*" he barks, and heads for the bathroom. "Jesus Christ, I'll be *fine!*" He goes in. Slams the door.

I hear him turn on the shower. I think, *Give the boy privacy, space.* I pick up the plastic ice bucket beside the TV. The trailer for *As Good as It Gets* is playing, as it did at the Menger—Greg Kinnear asking Jack Nicholson, "Do you know where you're lucky?"

This evening I do.

I walk downstairs and tuck the ice bucket under the stainless-steel spout of the motel's ice machine. I press the button. Ice falls like a jackpot. I feel luckier than I've felt in my life. Because of this road trip, I have my son back. Something in him has healed, and I know he'll be okay. Oh, I don't know the details—that his Ultimate team will take off at Maclay and he'll reconnect with his friends and be accepted at Brown and make their A Ultimate team when he's just a freshman, but before he leaves home for college he'll burst in the door in his bright blue cap and gown after Maclay's graduation and laugh because friends and family are giving him a standing ovation, and I'll stand there thinking, *I've never seen him so happy*, and after college he'll marry the love of his life, Caroline, and they'll have two darling daughters, Harper and Samantha, and maybe he'll take them on road trips and tell them our family story. I don't know any of this. I just know he'll be fine.

I carry the ice up the stairs. At the top, on the breezeway, I'm struck by the field to the north. The wind is blowing the golden-lit grass so it lies one direction, like the hair on Granddaddy's arm.

I set down the bucket and lean on the rail.

The year my father was dying, I asked him what he thought of Granddaddy.

"He was a mean son-of-a-bitch," he said, then he softened. "He couldn't connect."

At the end of the day, that's all that matters.

I wonder who Granddaddy might have been if his parents had raised him with kindness. I wonder who Mamaw might have been if her parents had given her the love and attention she needed. Big Mama had seven children, who nearly starved because Big Dada spent all his money saving his soul. No wonder Mamaw held onto her shiny objects.

Or maybe we all do. Maybe we all have something we won't let go of that limits our Self and our freedom. "What hinders you?" asked the Stoics. I quit the work that I love because I kept hitting walls. It felt fruitless. I felt like a failure. But isn't it enough to follow my bliss and, when it doesn't feel blissful, to confront—and overcome—my anxiety, fear?

The wind dies down. I think of Granddaddy, who threw in the towel, and Ross and my mother, who didn't. And I decide to start writing again.

The golden light goes, leaving a lavender sky. "Last light," my mother calls it. Soon it will be the blue hour. I feel grateful to her for giving me a childhood that wasn't traumatic. For bringing me to this small Texas town. I think of that day she knew she could do it, how she walked down the diving board on her hands. Maybe that's what parenting is—walking on hands. Trying to keep our lives—and our children's—in balance. Now and then, if we're lucky, we get it right.

To the north I see the first faint stars of Cassiopeia—that Running W in the sky. The grass ripples like water. A freshet, my father called it when we went sailing—a signal that wind's rushing toward us. Like time. Something you tighten into.

I hold on to the cool metal rail and tighten into the future. I feel the wind on my face. I feel peace, gratitude, joy. I feel free. But most of all I feel lucky. My life feels like an unexpected gift—one meaning, I remember, of grace.

Acknowledgments

Gratitude is a gift to the grateful, so I'm twice blessed by the generosity of heart and time and talent of everyone who has helped me bring this book into being:

Cal Barksdale, you truly are the best editor ever. Thank you for your kindness, patience, brilliant problem solving, and impeccable taste. Working with you on the book has been the happiest publishing experience of my writing life. And thanks to your assistant, Amy Singh, production editor Jordan Koluch, cover designer Erin Seaward-Hiatt, and to my copy editor, Katherine Enderle, for your kind, gentle hand. If the book is beautiful—and it is, beyond my wildest dreams—I owe it to all of you.

Jay Cassell, an editorial director at Skyhorse Publishing: thank you for responding to my query letter with music to a writer's ears—"Sounds like quite the memoir"—and for bringing the manuscript to Cal Barksdale's attention.

My dear friend, fellow writer, Nova Scotia neighbor, trainer, and workout buddy, Charles Gaines: thanks for suggesting, during one of our workouts, that I query Jay Cassell about this memoir.

My darling (or should I say "dahling"?) writing partner, Matt Stevens: thanks for our long, happy writing partnership and our "enduring friendship," as you so beautifully put it not long ago—and for helping me craft that query letter to Jay Cassell.

My daughter-in-law, Caroline Pitt Loomis: profound gratitude for reading an early version of the manuscript and for taking the cover photo of Ross and me so many years ago—and finding the photo in a box in your attic.

My dearest childhood friend and fellow tomboy, Ann Owens, now Tilton: thanks for inviting me to climb the mesquite tree in your backyard so we could bare our souls and tell each other what we wanted to be. And for posing with me for the mud photo.

Very special thanks to Ormond Loomis, for tracking down the mud photo.

And thanks to my gal pals Virginia Scruggs and Tiiu Poder, for reading and loving the manuscript—and for your invaluable insights.

The book would not have been written at all without the early encouragement of three writers:

My hilarious friend, the late and greatly missed Stuart Hample, who exclaimed shortly after Ross and I returned from our road trip, "That's your next book!"

Mary Pipher, who answered the letter I wrote her nineteen years ago with five unforgettable and inspiring words, "You must write this book!"

Terry Tempest Williams, who deepened my vision of what the book could be when I worked with her as a Nonfiction Fellow at Breadloaf Writers Conference.

I cannot thank you enough.

And I could not have written this memoir if it weren't for the support of my beautiful, brilliant, bighearted family—Anne, Ethan, Blake, and Eliot Thompson, Ross, Caroline, Harper, and Samantha Loomis, and my sister and brother-in-law, Pat and Mark Sellergren. Eternal gratitude to all of you for putting me up and putting up with me and for your input as I worked on the manuscript, cover, title, and subtitle of the book. And Pat, thanks for being the best big sister ever, for riding shotgun through our childhood and beyond, and for confirming and clarifying my family memories.

As I was typing these gratitudes, my daughter, Anne, texted me from the rose garden at the Woodland Park Zoo in Seattle, sending a photo of her son, Blake, now five, in front of a yellow rose bush. She had just told him that yellow roses were my favorite, and she texted what Blake said, "Maybe yellow roses are her favorite because yellow is my favorite and she loves me!" I do. More than the stars and the moon and the pizza in the pan, as we love to say in our family. You and Eliot and Harper and Samantha and your wonderful parents are the loves—and the light—of my life. Thanks to all of you for being my inspiration for writing this book and preserving our family story.

And my deepest gratitude to my son, Ross, who refused to read the memoir until it was in page proofs (and, yes, I was a wreck while he read it). But when he finished the book he said, "This is a love letter from a mother to a son." It is. Thank you for wanting to spend spring break with your mother when you were sixteen.